Shakespeare For Kids:

Four plays adapted to perform with kids

Romeo and Juliet
Julius Caesar
Midsummer Night's Dream
Macbeth

Adapted by CC Beechum
By William Shakespeare

Other books written by CC Beechum

Penelope Barrows #1 The Case of the Blowing Whistle
Penelope Barrows #2 The Case of the Red Sneaker
Penelope Barrows #3 The Case of the Poison Pen Letter

Shakespeare for Kids: Romeo and Juliet
Shakespeare for Kids: Julius Caesar
Shakespeare for Kids: Macbeth
Shakespeare for Kids: Midsummer Night's Dream
(Out in spring 2013.)

Recommended for Young Adult Readers

Published by Ebenezer Publishing Co.

ISBN- 13: 978-1478263364
ISBN-10: 1478263369

Dedication

To every drama club class that ever performed with me, every performance enriched my life, as I hope it did yours

A Book of Plays

Let me begin by saying that all the lines used in the following plays are for the most part verbatim Shakespeare, with a twist here or there. Most of the line is in there, but some were just too long or too confusing for youngsters, so they've been shortened to facilitate use. Some parts are intentionally left out. The main gist of the play is in there, the most important part. Kids love to use these words, it makes them feel important. I would like to believe that Willie would not be upset.

These plays are designed to have a group of children perform them. They take approximately sixty to eighty minutes each play, with a fifteen-minute intermission thrown in. You can however make them shorter or longer if you prefer to. Don't forget about the curtains, stagehands, set designers and a stage manager. These parts are very important in a production of any kind. Some parts can be deleted or added. It's your performance, tailor it to your specific needs. Not everyone wants to be the center of attraction. (Wink,wink.)

I have performed these plays many times, with very diverse groups of children. Each time it was most enjoyable. I have included some stage directions also, please feel free to do whatever you want with them, use them or not. Use your imagination wildly, because the children will definitely use theirs.

And.......action!!!

Romeo and Juliet
Cast of Characters

Benvolio

Romeo

Paris

Nurse

Juliet

Lady Capulet

Capulet

Friar

Mercutio

Stage Manager

Tybalt

Curtains

Balthazar

Apothecary

Narrator

Servingmen

Musicians

Party Guests

Stagehands

Romeo and Juliet

Enter Narrator

NARRATOR. The time is the 15th century. The place is Verona, Italy. The Montagues and the Capulets, two noble families, have long disturbed the city's peace, with their senseless feud.

At their home, the Capulets are preparing for a masked ball to celebrate the forthcoming marriage of fourteen-year old Juliet Capulet to Count Paris. Romeo Montague, crashes the Capulet party with his friend Mercutio. When Romeo sees Juliet there, he falls desperately in love. Juliet returns his feelings, and the two speak of love in the famous balcony scene. Although their parents do not know that they have even met, they plan to marry.

Friar Lawrence performs the ceremony secretly. After the wedding Juliet returns home. The friar hopes the marriage will end the feud.

Meanwhile, Tybalt, Juliet's cousin provokes Mercutio and has a quarrel with him and kills him. Romeo rushes to defend his friend and kills Tybalt. The Prince of Verona banishes Romeo in punishment for his crime.

The next morning Juliet's father insists she marry Paris. Juliet begs Friar Lawrence for help. He gives her a potion that masks death. Later she awakens in the Capulet burial vault.

Romeo fails to receive Friars letters telling him of the plan. Thinking Juliet is really dead, he buys a vial of poison and goes to the Capulet tomb. There he drinks the poison and dies.

Waking from her coma, Juliet sees Romeo dead, and snatching the dagger from his belt, she kills herself. Their deaths bring the Capulets and the Montagues to their senses. Grief stricken they finally make peace.

You can either put this in the program, or have the Narrator read it. Then you can have them change position to start the play.

(Beginning of play.)

Enter Narrator

NARRATOR. Two households, both alike in dignity, In the fair Verona, where we lay our scene, From ancient grudge break to new mutiny, Where civil blood makes civil hands unclean. From forth the fatal loins of these two foes A pair of star-crossed lovers take their life. Whose misadventures piteous overthrows Doth with their death bury their parents strife. The fearful passage of their death-marked love, And the continuance of their parents rage, Which, but their children's end, naught could remove, Is now the two hours traffic of our stage: The which if you with patient ears attend, What here shall miss, our toil shall strive to mend.

Exit Narrator

Act One
Scene One
Verona, a public place

Enter Romeo and Benvolio

BENVOLIO. Good Morrow, cousin.

ROMEO. Is the day so young?

BENVOLIO. But new struck nine.

ROMEO. Ay me, sad hours seem long. Was that my father that went hence so fast.

BENVOLIO. It was. What lengthens Romeo's hours?

ROMEO. Not having that which, having, makes them short.

BENVOLIO. In love?

ROMEO. Out.

BENVOLIO. Of love?

ROMEO. Out of her favor where I am in love.

BENVOLIO. Alas that love so gentle in his view Should be so tyrannous and rough in proof.

ROMEO. Alas that love, whose view is muffled still, should without eyes see pathways to his will! Where shall we dine? O me! This love feel I that feel no love in this. Dost thou not laugh?

BENVOLIO. No coz, I rather weep.

ROMEO. Good heart at what?

BENVOLIO. At thy good heart's oppression.

ROMEO. Why such is love's transgression. Love is a smoke made with the fume of sighs. A madness most discreet, A choking gall, and a preserving sweet. Farewell, my coz.

BENVOLIO. Soft, I will go along; And if you leave me so, you do me wrong?

ROMEO. Tut, I have lost myself. I am not here. This is not Romeo. He's some other where.

BENVOLIO. Tell me in sadness who is that you love?

ROMEO. What, shall I groan and tell thee?

BENVOLIO. Groan? Why no, but sadly tell me who.

ROMEO. In sadness, cousin, I do love a woman.

BENVOLIO. A right fair mark, fair coz, is soonest hit. Be ruled by me. Forget to think of her.

ROMEO. O teach me how I should forget to think.

BENVOLIO. By giving liberty unto thine eyes. Examine other beauties.

ROMEO. (Shakes head in agreement.) 'Tis the way. But he that is stricken blind cannot forget. Show me a mistress that is passing fair. Farewell, thou canst not teach me to forget.

BENVOLIO. I'll pay that doctrine or else die in debt.

Exit Romeo and Benvolio

Act One
Scene Two
Capulet Home

Enter Nurse and Lady Capulet

LADY CAPULET. Nurse, where's my daughter?

NURSE. I bade her come. Juliet, God forbid where are you? Where's that girl? What Juliet!

Enter Juliet

JULIET. How now who calls?

NURSE. Your mother.

JULIET. Madam, I am here, what is your will?

LADY CAPULET. This is the matter. Nurse, give leave awhile, we must talk in secret. (Waves her hand away at nurse.) Nurse, come back again. Thou knowest my daughter's of a pretty age.

NURSE. (Shaking her head in agreement.) On Lammas Eve at night she shall be fourteen. That she shall marry? How long is it now to Lammas Eve?

LADY CAPULET. A fortnight and odd days.

NURSE. Even or odd, of all days in the year, come Lammas Eve she shall be fourteen.

LADY CAPULET. Enough of this, I pray thee, hold thy peace.

NURSE. Yes Madam.

LADY CAPULET. Marry, that marry is the very theme I came to talk of. Tell she, daughter Juliet, How stands your disposition to be married?

JULIET. It is an honor that I dream not of.

NURSE. An honour! Were not thine only nurse, I would say thou hadst sucked wisdom from thine air.

LADY CAPULET. Well, think of marriage now. Younger that you here in Verona, ladies of esteem, are made already mothers. The valiant Paris seeks you for his love.

NURSE. A man, young lady! Lady, such a man as all the world-why he's perfect!

LADY CAPULET. What say you, can you love the gentleman? This night you shall behold him at our feast. So shall you share all that he doth possess. By having him making yourself no less.

JULIET. I'll look to like, if looking liking move; But no more deep will I endart mine eye, than your consent gives strength to make fly.

Enter Servingman

SERVINGMAN. Madam, The guests are come, supper serv'd up, you call'd, my young lady ask'd for, the nurse curs'd. (He throws his hands up in frustration.) I must hence to wait. I beseech you follow straight.

LADY CAPULET. We follow thee, come Juliet.

Exit Servingman

NURSE. Go, girl, seek happy nights to happy days.

Exit All

Act One
Scene Three
Capulet Home
Party

Enter Romeo, Mercutio, Benvolio, party guests, (Bearing gifts.) Capulet, Lady Capulet, Juliet, Nurse

Servingman come forth with napkins, etc, they place on a large buffet table, gifts are placed there also.

CAPULET. Welcome, gentlemen, ladies that have their toes. Which of you all will now deny to dance? Welcome gentlemen. You are welcome, gentlemen: come, musicians, play. A hall, a hall, give room! And foot it girls!

Music plays and they dance. (This can be fun and can go on for as long as you want.)

ROMEO. (To Servingman.) What lady's that which doth enrich the hand of yonder night?

SERVINGMAN. I know not, sir.

ROMEO. O, doth teach the torches to burn bright! It seems she hangs upon the cheek of the night. Did my heart love till now? Forswear it, sight. Nor I ne'r saw true beauty till this night.

TYBALT. This by his voice should be a Montague. What, dares the slave. Now by the stock and honor of my kin, to strike him dead I hold it not a sin.

CAPULET. Why how now kinsman, wherefore storm you so?

TYBALT. Uncle, this is a Montague, our foe: A villain that is hither come in spite To scorn at our solemn night.

CAPULET. Young Romeo is it?

TYBALT. 'Tis he, that villain Romeo.

CAPULET. Content thee, gentle coz, let him alone. And, to say truth, Verona brags of him To be a virtuous and well governed youth. I would not for the wealth of all this town Here in my house do him harm. Therefore, be patient, take no note of him.

TYBALT. It fits when such a villain is a guest. I'll not endure him.

CAPULET. He shall be endured. What, Goodsman boy! I say he shall! Go to! Am I the master here, or you? Go to! You'll not endure him? God mend my soul! You'll make mutiny among my guests!

TYBALT. Why, uncle, 'tis a shame.

CAPULET. Go to, go to! You are a saucy boy. Be quiet, or-More light, more light! I'll make you quiet; what!

TYBALT. I will withdraw; but this intrusion shall, Now seeming sweet, convert to bitt'rest gall.

Exit Tybalt

ROMEO. (To Juliet, taking her hand in his.) If I profane with my unworthiest hand This holy shrine: My lips, two blushing pilgrims, ready stand To smooth that rough touch with a tender kiss. (He kisses her hand.)

JULIET. Good pilgrim, you do wrong your hand too much, For saints have hands that pilgrims' hands do touch, And palm to palm is holy palmers' kiss. (They touch hands palm to palm or kiss, depending on age.)

ROMEO. O, then, dear saint, let lips do what hands do! (Palm to palm, or kiss.)

JULIET. Then have my lips the sin that they took.

ROMEO. Sin from my lips? O trespass sweetly urg'd! Give me my sin again. (Kiss.)

JULIET. You kiss by th' book.

NURSE. Madam, your mother craves a word with you.

ROMEO. What is her mother?

NURSE. Marry, bachelor, Her mother is the lady of the house. And a good lady, and a wise and virtuous. I tell you, he that can lay hold of her Shall have chinks. (Money.)

ROMEO. Is she a Capulet? O dear account! My life is my foe's debt.

CAPULET. (To Romeo and Benvolio who are about to leave.) Nay, gentleman, prepare not to be gone; We have a trifling foolish banquet towards. (They beg off.) Is it e'en so? Why then, I thank you all. I thank you, honest gentlemen. Good night. More torches here!

Exit all, but Juliet, and Nurse

JULIET. Come hither, Nurse. What is yon gentleman? (Pointing to Romeo and Benvolio leaving.)

NURSE. The son and heir of old Tiberio.

JULIET. What's he that now is going out of door? (Pointing to the guests leaving.)

NURSE. Marry, that I think be young Petruchio.

JULIET. What's he that follows there, that would not dance?

NURSE. I know not.

JULIET. Go ask his name.- If he be married, My grave is like to be my wedding bed.

NURSE. His name is Romeo, and a Montague, The only son of your great enemy.

JULIET. My only love, sprung from my only hate! Too early seen unknown, and known too late! Prodigious (Monstrous.) birth of love it is to me That I must love a loathed enemy.

NURSE. What's this? What's this?

JULIET. A rhyme I learn'd even now Of one I danc'd withal.

Someone calls for Juliet off stage.

NURSE. Anon, anon! Come, let's away; the strangers all are gone.

Exit Nurse and Juliet

Act Two
Scene One
Capulet's Orchard

Enter Romeo

ROMEO. Can I go forward when my heart is here? Turn back dull earth!

Enter Benvolio and Mercutio
Opposite stage they don't see each other.

BENVOLIO. Romeo! My cousin, Romeo! Romeo! (Obviously looking for Romeo.)

MERCUTIO. He is wise, and, on my life, hath he stolen him home to bed.

BENVOLIO. He ran this way, and leapt this orchard wall. Call,good Mercutio.

MERCUTIO. Romeo, Romeo!! (They leave.)

ROMEO. (Kneeling.) (Enter Juliet she is on a balcony, Romeo is hidden from her view.) But soft, what light through yonder window breaks? It is the east and Juliet is the sun! Arise fair sun and kill the envious moon Who is already sick and pale with grief That thou her maid are far more fair than she. It is my lady, O it is my love! O that she knew she were! She speaks, yet she says nothing. What of that? See how she leans her cheek upon her hand, (Juliet leans her cheek upon her hand.) O that I were a glove upon that hand. That I might touch that cheek!

JULIET. Ay me!

ROMEO. O speak again bright angel, for thou art as glorious to this night, being o'er my head.

JULIET. O Romeo, Romeo, wherefore art thou Romeo? Deny thy father and refuse thy name. And I'll no longer be a Capulet.

ROMEO. Shall I hear more, or shall I speak at this? (She can see him now.)

JULIET. 'Tis but thy name is my enemy; Thou art thyself, though not a Montague. What's a Montague? It is nor hand, nor foot, nor arm, nor face, nor any other part belonging to a man. O be some other name. What's in a name? That which we call a rose by any other word would smell as sweet. So Romeo would, were he not Romeo called, retain that dear title.

ROMEO. I take thee at thy word. Call me but love, and I'll be newly baptized: Henceforth I never will be Romeo.

JULIET. Art thou not Romeo, and a Montague?

ROMEO. By a name I know not how to tell thee who I am.

JULIET. How cam'st thou hither, tell me, and wherefore? The orchard walls are high and hard to climb. If any of my kinsmen see thee they will murder thee.

ROMEO. I have night's cloak to hide me from their eyes. And but thou love me, let them find me here. My life were better ended by their hate.

JULIET. But to be frank I wish for the thing I have. My love is as deep as the sea. The more I have, for both are infinite. I hear some noise within. Dear love, adieu. (Nurse calls Juliet within.) Anon, good nurse! Sweet Montague be true. Stay but a little, I will come again.

Exit Juliet

ROMEO. O blessed, blessed night. I am afeard. Being in night, all this is but a dream.

Enter Juliet again

JULIET. Three words, dear Romeo, and good night indeed. Thy purpose marriage, send me word tomorrow. And all my fortunes at thy foot I'll lay, and follow thee my lord throughout the world.

NURSE. Madam! (From within.)

JULIET. I come anon-but if thou meanest not well-I do beseech thee-

NURSE. Madam!

JULIET. Tomorrow will I send.

ROMEO. So thrive my soul-

JULIET. A thousand times goodnight.

Exit Juliet (She turns around to go.)

ROMEO. A thousand times the worse, to want thy light.

JULIET. Romeo!

ROMEO. My dear?

JULIET. What o'clock tomorrow shall I send to thee?

ROMEO. By the hour of nine.

JULIET. I will not fail. 'Tis twenty years till then.

ROMEO. I would I were thy bird.

JULIET. Good night, good night! Parting is such sweet sorrow That I shall say good night till it be morrow.

ROMEO. Would I were sleep and peace, so sweet to rest!

Act Two Scene Two
Friar Lawrence's Garden
Friar in garden

Enter Romeo

ROMEO. Good morrow father!

FRIAR. Benedicte! What early tongue so sweet saluteth me? Where hast thou been?

ROMEO. I have been feasting with mine enemy, Where on a sudden, my heart's dear love is set on the fair daughter of rich Capulet, so hers is set on mine. We met, we wooed, and made exchange of vow. But this I pray. That thou consent to marry us today.

FRIAR. Holy Saint Francis! What a change is here!

ROMEO. I pray thee chide me not. Her I love now.

FRIAR. But, come young waverer, come go with me, In one respect I'll thy assistant be. For this alliance may so happy be.

ROMEO. O, let us hence; I stand on sudden haste.

Friar marries Romeo and Juliet.
I usually do this scene as a silent one in front of the curtain, whilst' the scene is changed backstage.

Open curtain.

A street
Enter Benvolio and Mercutio

MERCUTIO. Where the devil can Romeo be? Came he not home tonight?

BENVOLIO. Not to his father's. I spoke with his man. Tybalt, the kinsman to old Capulet, hath sent a letter to his father's house.

MERCUTIO. A challenge on my life.

BENVOLIO. Romeo will answer it.

MERCUTIO. Any man that can write may answer a letter.

BENVOLIO. Nay, he will answer the letter's master, how he dares, being dared.

Enter Romeo

BENVOLIO. Here comes Romeo, here he comes.

ROMEO. Good morrow to you both.

MERCUTIO. Romeo, Tybalt has made a challenge on my life.

ROMEO. Why, what is Tybalt?

MERCUTIO. He's the courageous captain of compliments, he fights as you sing.

ROMEO. I will answer it. I will encounter Tybalt.

Mercutio and Benvolio leave.
Enter Tybalt, and a silent scene ensues between Romeo and Tybalt.
Romeo kills Tybalt in a battle.
(You do not have to make this silent.)

Act Three
Scene One
Capulet home

Juliet on stage.

JULIET. (Pacing.) The clock struck nine when I did send the nurse: in half an hour she promised to return. Perchance she cannot meet him. Oh, that's not so. Is three long hours, yet she is not come. O, she is lame.

Enter Nurse, running

JULIET. Now, good sweet nurse-O Lord thou sad?

NURSE. I am aweary! Give me leave awhile. Fie, how my bones ache! What a jaunt have I had! (She sits.)

JULIET. Nay, come I pray thee speak. Good, nurse, speak!

NURSE. What haste! Can you not see that I am out of breath?

JULIET. How art thou out of breath? Is thy news good or bad? Answer to that. Let me be satisfied, isn't good or bad?

NURSE. Well, you have made a simple choice! You know not how to choose a man. Romeo! No, not he. He is not the flower of courtesy. Go thy ways, wench, serve God.

JULIET. No, no. But all this did I know. What says he of our marriage? What of that?

NURSE. Lord, how my head aches! What a head have I! Your love says like an honest gentleman, and a courteous, and a kind, and a handsome, and, I warrant, a virtuous- Where is your mother?

JULIET. Where is my mother? Why, she is within. Where should she be? How oddly thou repliest! Ay me! What news?

NURSE. Ah well-a-day, he's dead, he's dead, he's dead!! We are undone, lady, we are undone. Alack the day, he's gone, he's killed, he's dead!

JULIET. Can heaven be so envious?

NURSE. Romeo can, though heaven cannot. O Romeo, Romeo, Who ever would have thought it? Romeo!

JULIET. What devil art thou that dost torment me thus? Hath Romeo slain Himself? If he be slain say 'Ay,' or if not, 'No.'

NURSE. I saw the wound, I saw it with mine eyes-Pale, pale as ashes. All in gore-blood. I swooned at the sight.

JULIET. O break, my heart. Break at once.

NURSE. O Tybalt, Tybalt the best friend I had. O courteous Tybalt! Honest gentleman! That ever I should live to see thee dead. Tybalt is gone, and Romeo banished. Romeo that killed him, he is banished.

JULIET. O God! Did Romeo's hand shed Tybalt's blood? My dearest cousin? And my dearer lord? For who is living if those two are gone?

NURSE. It did, it did, alas the day it did. There's no trust, No faith, no honesty in men. Shame come to Romeo!

JULIET. Blistered be thy tongue! For such a wish! He was not born to shame. Oh, what a beast was I to chide at him!

NURSE. Will you speak well of him that killed your cousin?

JULIET. Shall I speak ill of him that is my husband? Back, foolish tears, back to your native spring. My husband lives, that Tybalt would have slain, And Tybalt's dead, that would have slain my husband. Where is my father and my mother, Nurse?

NURSE. Weeping and wailing over Tybalt's corse. Will you go to them? I will bring you thither.

JULIET. Both you and I, for Romeo is exiled. O, find him! Give this ring to my true knight, And bid him come to take his last farewell. (Juliet gives her a ring.)

Exit both, opposite stage of each other

NARRATOR. (In front of curtain.) Juliet's mother and father want Juliet to marry Paris on Thursday. It is Tuesday. Juliet cannot talk her parents out of it. Juliet decides to go to Friar Lawrence for his help.

Act Three
Scene Two
Friar Lawrence's Garden (In front of curtain.)

Enter Juliet

JULIET. Tell me not, Friar that thou hearest of this. If in thy wisdom thou canst give no help. And with this knife I'll help it presently. (Shows him a knife.) God joined my heart and Romeo's in your hands.

FRIAR. Hold daughter. I do spy a kind of hope. If, rather than to marry County Paris, Thou hast the strength of will to slay thyself, An if thou darest, I'll give thee remedy.

JULIET. O, bid me leap, rather than marry Paris, And I will do it without fear or doubt, To live an unstained wife to my sweet love.

FRIAR. Hold, then. Go home, be merry. Give consent to marry Paris. Wednesday is tomorrow. Tomorrow night look that thou lie alone. (Shows her a vial.) Take thou this vial, being then in bed, And this liquor drink thou off, When presently through all thy veins shall run A cold and drowsy humor, for no pulse Shall, stiff and stark and cold, appear like death And then awake as from a pleasant sleep. In the meantime, against thou shalt awake, Shall Romeo by my letters know our drift, And hither shall he come.

JULIET. Give me, give me! O, tell not me of fear!

FRIAR. Hold. Get you gone. Be strong and prosperous In this resolve. I'll send a friar with speed To Mantua with my letters to thy lord.

JULIET. Love give me strength, and strength shall help afford. Farewell, dear Father. (Friar leaves, open curtain to Capulet home.) Farewell! God knows when we shall meet again. (She drinks the contents of the vial.) I have faint cold fear thrills through my veins. What if the poison which the Friar has giveth me makes me dead? Romeo, I come! This drink to thee.

Capulet Home

Juliet lies down and goes to sleep. (I usually spilt the stage.)

Enter Nurse and Lady Capulet

CAPULET. Go waken Juliet; go and trim her up. I'll go and chat with Paris. Hie, make haste, make haste. The bridegroom he is come already. Make haste I say.

NURSE. (She goes to wake her up.) Mistress! What, mistress! Juliet! Why, lamb! Why, lady! The County Paris hath set up his rest How sound is she asleep! I need must wake her.—Madam, madam, madam! What, dressed and in your clothes, and down again? Must needs wake you. Lady, lady, lady! (She kneels over her to listen to her heart, she takes her hand.)—Alas, alas! Help, help! My lady's dead!—Oh, well-a-day, that ever I was born!—My lord! My lady!

LADY CAPULET. What noise is here?

NURSE. O lamentable day!

LADY CAPULET. What is the matter? (She bends over Juliet taking her pulse.)

NURSE. She's dead, deceased, she's dead. Alack the day!

LADY CAPULET. Alack the day. She's dead, she's dead, she's dead! (She puts her head in her hands and begins to cry.)

CAPULET. Ha? Let me see her. Out, alas! She's cold. Her blood is settled, and her joints are stiff. Death lies on her like an untimely frost. (He takes her hand in his.)

NURSE. O lamentable day!

LADY CAPULET. O woeful time.

Enter Friar and Paris

FRIAR. Come, is the bride ready to go to church?

CAPULET. Ready to go, but never to return. O son! The night before thy wedding day Hath death lain with thy wife.

PARIS. Most detestable Death, by thee beguiled. O love! O life! Not life, but love in death.

CAPULET. Uncomfortable time, why camest thou now. Alack, my child is dead, And with my child my joys are buried.

FRIAR LAWRENCE. Sir, go you in, and, madam, go with him; And go, Sir Paris. Every one prepare To follow this fair corse unto her grave.

Exit all except Friar, he stays with the body

Act Four
Scene One
In front of Capulet home

Enter Romeo

ROMEO. I dreamt my lady came and found me dead- strange dream that gives a dead man time to think. (Enter Balthazar.) News from Verona? How, now Balthasar, Dost thou bring me letters from Friar? How doth my lady? Is my father well? How fares my Juliet?

BALTHAZAR. Then she is well, and nothing can be ill. Her body sleeps in Capels' monument, And her immortal part with angels lives. I saw her laid low in her kindred's vault And presently took post to tell it you.

ROMEO. Is it e'en so? Then I defy you, stars! Get me ink and paper,
And hire post horses. I will hence tonight.

BALTHAZAR. I do beseech you, sir, have patience. Your looks are pale and wild, and do import Some misadventure.

ROMEO. Tush, thou art deceived. Leave me and do the thing I bid thee do. Hast thou no letters to me from the Friar?

BALTHAZAR. No, my good lord.

ROMEO. No matter. Get thee gone, And hire those horses. I'll be with thee straight.

Exit Balthazar

ROMEO. Well, Juliet, Let's see for means. To enter in the thoughts of desperate men! I do remember an apothecary—And hereabouts he dwells. "An if a man did need a poison now"—(Thinking aloud.) As I remember, this should be the house. What, ho! Apothecary!

Knocks on Apothecary door.

APOTHECARY. Who calls so loud!

ROMEO. Come hither, man. I see that thou art poor. Hold, there is forty ducats. Let me have A dram of poison.

APOTHECARY. Such mortal drugs I have, but Mantua's law Is death to any he that utters them.

ROMEO. The world is not thy friend nor the world's law. (Holds out money.)

APOTHECARY. My poverty, but not my will, consents.

ROMEO. I pay thy poverty and not thy will.

APOTHECARY. (Gives Romeo poison.) Put this in any liquid thing you will And drink it off; and, if you had the strength Of twenty men, it would dispatch you straight.

ROMEO. (Gives Apothecary the money.) There is thy gold, worse poison to men's souls, To Juliet's grave, for there must I use thee.

Exit Apothecary and Romeo

Act Four
Scene Two
Capulets Vault

This is a dramatic last scene and should be drawn out.
Enter Romeo
Juliet lying still.
Romeo sees Juliet, goes to her, thinking her dead he drinks the contents of the vial.
He dies.
Juliet rises.

Enter Friar

JULIET. O comfortable Friar! Where is my lord? I do remember well where I should be, And there I am. Where is my Romeo?

FRIAR LAWRENCE: I hear some noise. Lady, come from that nest Come, come away. Thy husband in thy bosom there lies dead (Points to Romeo.) Stay not to question, for the watch is coming. Come, go, good Juliet. I dare no longer stay.

JULIET. Go, get thee hence, for I will not away.

Exit Friar Lawrence

JULIET. What's here? A cup, closed in my true love's hand? Poison, I see, hath been his timeless end.—O churl, drunk all, and left no friendly drop To help me after? I will kiss thy lips. Haply some poison yet doth hang on them. (She bends over and kisses his lips.) Yea, noise? Then I'll be brief. O happy dagger, This is thy sheath. There rust and let me die. (Stabs herself with Romeo's dagger that she snatches from his belt and dies, they lie beside each other.)

THE END

Julius Caesar

Cast of Characters

Flavius

Marullus

Citizens

Caesar

Calpurnia (Caesar's wife.)

Soothsayer

Artemidorus

Portia (Brutus' wife.)

Narrator

Lucius (Servant.)

Stage Manager

Stagehands

Curtains

Conspirators:

Antony

Decius

Brutus

Cassius

Casca

Cinna

Decius

Julius Caesar

Enter Narrator

NARRATOR. Julius Caesar is set in Rome. The action begins on February 15, 44 BC the day of the feast of Lupercal, a Roman festival. A fortune-teller is warning Roman ruler Julius Caesar to "beware the ides of March," the 15th. While he dismisses the fortune-teller as just a dreamer, the men who oppose Caesar, because of his ambition to be king, discuss killing him.

This scene is a short one. Caesar has just returned home in triumph after having defeated his rival, Pompey. The people have taken the day off from work to celebrate. You can make it longer if you wish.

(Beginning of play.)

Act One
Scene One
Rome A Public place

Enter Flavius, Marullus, and citizens of Rome

FLAVIUS. Hence! Home, you idle creatures, get you home. Is this a holiday? Being mechanical, you ought not walk upon a laboring day without the sign. What is your profession? Speak, what trade art thou?

CITIZEN 1. Why, sir, a carpenter.

MARULLUS. Where is thy leather apron and thy rule? What does thou with thy best apparel on? You, sir, what trade are you?

CITIZEN 2. Truly, sir, in respect of a fine workman, I am but, as you say, a cobbler.

MARULLUS. But what trade are thou? Answer me directly.

CITIZEN 2. A trade, sir with a safe conscience, a mender of bad soles.

FLAVIUS. What trade, thou knave? Thou naughty knave, what trade?

CITIZEN 2. I beseech you, sir, be not out with me: yet if you be out, sir, I can mend you.

MARULLUS. What meanest thou by that? Mend me, thou saucy fellow?

CITIZEN 2. Why, sir, cobble you.

FLAVIUS. Thou art a cobbler, art thou?

CITIZEN 2. Truly, sir, that I live by is with the awl.

FLAVIUS. But wherefore art not in thy shop today? Why dost thou lead these men about the streets.

CITIZEN 2. Truly, sir, to wear out their shoes, to get myself into more work. But indeed, sir, we make holiday to see Caesar and to rejoice in his triumph.

MARULLUS. Wherefore rejoice? What conquest brings he home? What tributaries (Captives.) follow him to Rome. You blocks, you stones, you worse than senseless things! O you hard hearts, you cruel men of Rome, knew you not Pompey? Be gone! Run to your houses, fall upon your knees, pray to the gods.

FLAVIUS. Go, go, good countrymen, and for this fault, assemble all the poor men of your sort and weep your tears.

Exit citizens

MARULLUS. May we do so? You know it is the feast of Lupercal.

FLAVIUS. It is no matter. Let no images be hung with Caesar's trophies. I'll about, and drive away the vulgars from the streets.

Act One
Scene Two
Rome a public place

Enter Caesar and Antony, dressed for the course. Calpurnia, Portia, Decius, Brutus, Cassius, Casca and Cinna. Soothsayer, citizens, Flavius, and Marullus follow

CAESAR. Calpurnia.

CASCA. Peace ho! Caesar speaks.

CAESAR. Calpurnia.

CALPURNIA. Here, my lord.

CAESAR. Stand you directly in Antony's way. Antonius.

ANTONY. Caesar, my lord?

CAESAR. Set on, and leave no ceremony out. (Music.)

SOOTHSAYER. (From the crowd.) Caesar!

CAESAR. Ha! Who calls?

CASCA. Bid every noise be still. Peace yet again! (Music ceases.)

CAESAR. Who is it in the press (Crowd.) that calls on me? I hear a tongue shriller than all the music cry Caesar! Speak: Caesar is turned to hear.

SOOTHSAYER. Beware the ides of March.

CAESAR. What man is that?

BRUTUS. A soothsayer bids you beware the ides of March.

CAESAR. Set him before me. Let me see his face.

CASSIUS. Fellow, come from the throng. Look upon Caesar. (Soothsayer comes from the throng.)

CAESAR. What sayest thou to me now? Speak once again.

SOOTHSAYER. Beware the ides of March.

CAESAR. He is a dreamer. Let us leave him. Pass. (He waves the soothsayer away.)

Trumpets. Exit all but Brutus and Cassius

CASSIUS. Will you go see the order of the course? (How the race is going.)

BRUTUS. Not I.

CASSIUS. I pray you do.

BRUTUS. I am not gamesome. I do lack some part of that quick spirit that is in Antony. Let me not hinder, Cassius, I'll leave you.

CASSIUS. Brutus, I do observe you now of late. You bear too stubborn and too strange a hand over a friend that loves you.

BRUTUS. Be not deceived. Vexed I am of late. Conceptions only proper to myself.

CASSIUS. Tell me, good Brutus, can you see your face?

BRUTUS. No, Cassius, for the eye sees not itself but by reflection, by some other things.

CASSIUS. 'Tis just, and it is very much lamented, Brutus, that you have no such mirrors that you might see your shadow.

BRUTUS. Into what dangers would you lead me, Cassius. That you would have me seek into myself for that which is not in me?

CASSIUS. Therefore, good Brutus, be prepared to hear.

BRUTUS. I do fear the people choose Caesar for their king.

CASSIUS. Ay, do you fear it? Then I must I think you would not have it so.

BRUTUS. I would not, Cassius; yet I love him well. I love the name of honor more than I fear death.

CASSIUS. I know that virtue to be in you, Brutus. I cannot tell what you and other men think of this life. I was born free as Caesar; so were you.

Act Two
Scene One
Rome
Brutus' house in his orchard

Enter Brutus

BRUTUS. What, Lucius, ho! I cannot, by the progress of the stars, give guess how near to day. Lucius, I say! I would it were my fault to sleep so soundly. When, Lucius, when? Awake. I say. What, Lucius!

Enter Lucius (Servant.)

LUCIUS. Called you, my lord?

BRUTUS. Get me a taper in my study.

LUCIUS. I will, my lord. (Exits to get candle.)

Enter Lucius

LUCIUS. The taper burneth in your closet, sir. This paper, thus sealed up: and I am sure it did not lie there when I went to bed. (He hands him the letter, I used a scroll.)

BRUTUS. Get you to bed again; it is not day. Is not tomorrow, boy, the ides of March?

LUCIUS. I know not sir.

BRUTUS. Look in the calendar, and bring me word.

LUCIUS. I will sir. (Exits to go look at calendar.)

BRUTUS. Brutus, thou sleepest. Awake! Shall Rome, stand under one man's awe? What, Rome?

LUCIUS. Sir, March is wasted fifteen days. (A knock is heard.)

BRUTUS. 'Tis good. Go to the gate, somebody knocks.

Exit Lucius

BRUTUS. Since Cassius first did whet me against Caesar, I have not slept.

Enter Lucius

LUCIUS. Sir, 'tis your brother Cassius at the door, Who doth desire to see you.

BRUTUS. Is he alone?

LUCIUS. No, sir, there are more with him.

BRUTUS. Do you know them?

LUCIUS. No, sir. Their hats are plucked about their ears and half their faces buried in their cloaks.

BRUTUS. Let 'em enter.

Exit Lucius

BRUTUS. O conspiracy, shamest thou to show thy dangerous brow by night.

Enter Cassius, Casca, Decius, and Cinna

CASSIUS. I think we are too bold upon your rest. Good morrow, Brutus. Do we trouble you?

BRUTUS. I have been up this hour, awake all night. Know I these men that come along with you?

CASSIUS. Yes, every man of them; and no man here. This is, Decius, Casca, and Cinna.

BRUTUS. They are all welcome. What watchful cares do interpose themselves betwixt your eyes and night?

CASSIUS. Shall I entreat a word?

Cassius and Brutus whisper aside.

DECIUS. Here lies the east. Doth not the day break here?

CASCA. No.

CINNA. O pardon, sir, it doth; and you gray lines that fret the clouds are messengers of day.

CASCA. You shall confess that you are both deceived. Here, as I point my sword, the sun arises.

BRUTUS. Give me your hands all over, one by one.

CASSIUS. And let us swear our resolution.

BRUTUS. No, not an oath. It shall be his judgment, Ceasar's, he ruled our hands. What other bond than secret Romans that have spoke the word and will not palter?

CASCA. Oh name him not!

CINNA. Then leave him out.

CASCA. Indeed he not fit!

DECIUS. Shall no man be touched, but only Caesar?

CASSIUS. Decius, well urged. I think it is not met Mark Antony, so well beloved of Caesar, should outlive Caesar. We shall find of him a shrewd contriver. Let Antony and Caesar fall together.

BRUTUS. Our course will seem too bloody. For Antony is but a limb of Caesar. Let's be sacrificers, but not butchers, Cassius. We all stand up against the spirit of Caesar, and in the spirit of men there is no blood.

CASSIUS. Yet, I fear him, for in the ingrafted love he bears Caesar.

BRUTUS. Alas, good Cassius, do not think of him. If he love Caesar, all that he can do is to himself. There is no fear in him. Let him not die, for he will live, and laugh at this hereafter.

Clock strikes three times.

BRUTUS. Peace, count the clock.

CASSIUS. The clock hath stricken three.

CASCA. 'Tis time to part.

Exit all but Brutus

Enter Portia

PORTIA. Brutus my lord.

BRUTUS. Portia! What mean you? Wherefore rise you now? It is not for your health thus to commit your weak condition to the raw cold morning.

PORTIA. Nor for yours either. You've urgently, Brutus, stole from my bed. And yesternight at supper you suddenly arose and walked about, musing and sighing with your arms across; and when I asked you what the matter was, you stared upon me with ungentle looks. It will not let you eat, nor talk, nor sleep. Make me acquainted with your cause of grief.

BRUTUS. I am not well in health, and that is all.

PORTIA. Brutus is wise, and were he not in health, he would embrace the means to come by it.

BRUTUS. Why, so I do. Good Portia, go to bed.

PORTIA. Is Brutus sick, and is it physical? Why you are heavy, and what men tonight have had resort to you? (Portia kneels.)

BRUTUS. Kneel not, gentle Portia. (He gives his hand out for her to rise.)

PORTIA. Tell me Brutus is it expected I should know no secrets that appertain to you?

BRUTUS. You are my true and honorable wife.

PORTIA. If this were true, then should I know this secret.

BRUTUS. O ye gods, render me worthy of this noble wife! Portia, go in awhile, and by and by thy shall partake the secrets of my heart. Leave me with haste.

Exit Portia

Act Two
Scene Two
Caesar's House
Thunder and Lightning

Enter Caesar in his nightgown pacing

CAESAR. Nor heaven nor earth have been at peace tonight. Thrice hath Calpurnia in her sleep cried out "help ho, they murder Caesar!" Who's within?

Enter servant

SERVANT. My lord?

CAESAR. Go bid the priests do present sacrifices, and bring me their opinions of success.

SERVANT. I will, my lord.

CALPURNIA. What mean you, Caesar? Think you to walk forth? You shall not stir out of the house today.

CAESAR. Caesar shall forth.

CALPURNIA. Caesar, I never stood on ceremonies, yet now they fright me. There is one within. O Caesar, these things are beyond all use, and I do fear them.

CAESAR. What can be avoided whose end is purposed by the mighty gods? Yet Caesar shall go forth, for these predictions are to the world in general as to Caesar.

CALPURNIA. Alas, my lord, your wisdom is consumed in confidence. Do not go forth today. Call it my fear that keeps you in the house, and not your own. We'll send

Mark Antony to the Senate House, and he shall say you are not well today. Let me upon my knee prevail in this. (She kneels.)

CAESAR. Mark Antony shall say I am not well, and for thy honor I will stay at home.

Enter Decius, Calpurnia rises

DECIUS. Caesar, all hail! Good morrow, worthy Caesar! I come to fetch you to the Senate House.

CAESAR. And you are come in very happy time to bear my greetings to the senators, and tell them that I will not come today. Cannot is false, I will not come today; tell them so, Decius.

CALPURNIA. Say he is sick.

CAESAR. Shall Caesar send a lie? To be afeared to tell greybeards the truth? Decius, go tell them: Caesar will not come.

DECIUS. Most mighty Caesar, let me know some cause. Lest I be laughed at when I tell them so.

CAESAR. The cause is my will, I will not come. Calpurnia here, my wife, stays me at home. She dreamt tonight she saw my statue, which, like a fountain with a hundred spouts, did run pure blood; and many lusty Romans came smiling and did bathe their hands in it.

DECIUS. The dream is all amiss interpreted; it was a vision fair and fortunate. Your statue spouting blood in many pipes, in which so many smiling Romans bathed, signifies that from you great Rome shall suck reviving blood and that great men shall press. This by Calpurnia's dream is signified.

CAESAR. And this way have you well expounded it.

DECIUS. And know it now-the Senate have concluded to give this day a crown to mighty Caesar. If you shall send them a word you will not come, their minds may change. If Caesar hide himself, shall they not whisper "Lo, Caesar is afraid"? Pardon me Caesar, for my dear dear love, bids me to tell you this.

CAESAR. How foolish do your fears seem now Calpurnia? I am ashamed I did yield to them. Give me my robe, for I will go.

Exit

Act Three
Scene One
Before the capitol

Enter Soothsayer, Artemidorus, Brutus, Caesar, Cassius, Casca, Decius, Antony, Cinna, and citizens.

CAESAR. The ides of March are come.

SOOTHSAYER. Ah, Caesar, but not gone.

ARTEMIDORUS. Hail, Caesar! Read this schedule. (Petition.)

DECIUS. Trebonius doth desire you to o'er read.

CAESAR. What touches us ourselves shall be last served.

ARTEMIDORUS. Delay not, Caesar! Read it instantly!

CAESAR. What, is that fellow mad?

CASSIUS. What, urge you your petition in the street? Come to the Capitol.

CAESAR. Are we all ready? What is now amiss that Caesar and his senate must redress?

BRUTUS. I kiss thy hand, but not in flattery, Caesar; desiring thee that Publius Cimber may have an immediate freedom of repeal.

CAESAR. What Brutus?

CASSIUS. Pardon, Caesar; Caesar, pardon. As low as to thy foot doth Cassius fall. To beg freedom for Publius Cimber.

CAESAR. I could be well moved, if I were as you; if I could pray to move, prayers would moe me. But I am constant as the northern star. That I was constant Cimber should be banished, and constant do remain to keep him so.

CINNA. O Caesar- (Kneeling near Caesar.)

CAESAR. Hence!

DECIUS. Great Caesar- (Kneeling near Caesar.)

CAESAR. Doth not Brutus bootless kneel?

CASCA. Speak, hands, for me.

They stab Caesar, Casca first, Brutus last.

CAESAR. Et tu, Brute? Then fall Caesar. (Dies.)

CINNA. Liberty! Freedom! Tyranny is dead! Run hence, proclaim, cry it about the streets.

CASSIUS. Some to the common pulpits, and cry out " Liberty, freedom!"

BRUTUS. People and senators, be not affrighted. Fly not, stand still. Ambition's debt is paid.

CASCA. Go to the pulpit, Brutus.

DECIUS. And Cassius too.

CASSIUS. Where is Antony?

CINNA. Fled to his house amazed. Men, wives, and children stare, cry out, and run as if were doomsday.

BRUTUS. Grant that, and then is death a benefit; so are we Caesar's friends, that have abridged his time of fearing death. Stoop, Romans, stoop, and let us bathe our hands in Caesar's blood. Up to our elbows. Then walk we forth to the market place, and waving our red o'er our heads, let's all cry, "peace, freedom, and liberty!"
(All stoop and wash in blood, I did this as just motions, no actual blood.)

DECIUS. What, shall we forth?

CASSIUS. Ay, every man away. Brutus shall lead, and we will grace his heels with the most boldest and best hearts of Rome.

Act Three
Scene Two
Before the capital

Enter Antony

BRUTUS. But here comes Antony. Welcome, Mark Antony.

ANTONY. O mighty Caesar! Dost thou lie so low! Are all thy conquests, glories, triumphs, spoils, shrunk to this measure? Fare thee well. I know not what you gentlemen intend, who else must be let blood, who else is rank?

BRUTUS. O Antony, beg not your death of us! Though now we must appear bloody and cruel, as by our hands, and this our present act. Our hearts you see not. They are pitiful.

CASSIUS. Your voice shall be as strong as any mans in the disposing of new dignities.

BRUTUS. Only be patient, till we have appeased the multitude, beside themselves with fear, and then we will deliver you the cause why I, that did love Caesar when I struck him, have thus proceeded.

ANTONY. I doubt not of your wisdom. Let each man render me his bloody hand. (They all grasp hands.) Gentleman all-alas, what shall I say?

CITIZEN 1. We will be satisfied! Let us be satisfied!

CITIZEN 2. I will hear Brutus speak.

BRUTUS. Mark Antony, here you take Caesar's body. You shall not in your funeral speech blame us, but speak all good you can devise of Caesar. If then that friend demand why Brutus rose against Caesar, this is my answer; not that I loved Caesar less but that I loved Rome more. Had you rather Caesar were living, and die all slaves, than that Caesar were dead, to live all free men? As Caesar loved me, I weep for him, but as he was ambitious I slew him.

ANTONY. Be it so. I do desire no more.

BRUTUS. Prepare the body then, follow us.

Exit all but Antony and citizens

CITIZEN 3. 'Twere best he speak no harm of Brutus here.

CITIZEN 1. This Caesar was a tyrant.

CITIZEN 2. We are blest that Rome is rid of him.

CITIZEN 3. Peace, let us hear what Antony can say.

ANTONY. Friends, Romans, countrymen, lend me your ears, I come to bury Caesar, not to praise him. The evil that men do lives after them, the good is oft interred with their bones; so be it with Caesar. The noble Brutus hath told you Caesar was ambitious; if it were so, it was a grievous fault, and grievously hath Caesar answered it. For Brutus is an honorable man, so are they all, all honorable men- Come I to speak in Caesar's funeral. He was my friend, faithful and just to me; but Brutus says he was ambitious, and Brutus is an honorable man. He hath brought many captives home to Rome. Did this in Caesar seem ambitious? When that the poor have cried, Caesar hath wept. Yet Brutus says he was ambitious, and Brutus is an honorable man. I thrice presented him the crown, which he did thrice refuse. Was this ambition? Yet Brutus says he was ambitious, and sure he is an honorable man. I speak not to disprove what Brutus spoke. But here I am to speak what I know. You did love him once, not without cause; what cause withholds you then to mourn for him? My heart is in the coffin there with Caesar, not with his murderers. I fear there will worse come in his place. And say to all the world, "This was a man!"

All citizens start talking, some yelling, they rush through the city after the true killers of Caesar.

THE END

Midsummer Night's Dream

Cast of Characters

Theseus-Duke of Athens

Bottom

Hippolyta- Queen of the Amazons

Egeus- Father of Hermia

Hermia- Daughter of Egeus, in love with Lysander

Lysander- Loved by Hermia

Helena- In love with Demetrius

Oberon- King of the Fairies

Titiana- Queen of the Fairies

Robin Goodfellow- A Puck (Fairy.)

Fairies 4-6 (Or whatever you choose.)

Attendants- For the King and Queen

Changeling

People at the wedding

Curtains

Narrator

Stage Manager

Midsummer Night's Dream

Enter Narrator

NARRATOR. There are four main strands to Midsummer Night's Dream. One, which forms the basis of the action, shows preparations for the marriage of, Theseus, Duke of Athens, to Hippolyta, Queen of the Amazons, and (In the last act.) its celebration. The second strand is the love story of Lysander and Hermia (Who elope to escape her father's opposition.) and of Demetrius. Shakespeare adds the comic complication of another girl (Helena.) jilted by, but still loving, one of the young men. The third strand is the play for the wedding. I did not include this strand, because the play would be just too long, but I did include the weddings of all the couples at the end of the play. Feel free to add this whole part in if you prefer. The fourth strand Shakespeare depicts a quarrel between Oberon and Titiana, King and Queen of the fairies. Oberon's attendant, Robin Goodfellow, a puck (Pixie.), interferes mischievously in the affairs of the lovers.

(Beginning of play.)

Act One
Scene One
At Hippolyta's castle

Enter Theseus, Hippolyta, and attendants

THESEUS. Now, fair Hippolyta, our nuptial hour draws apace. Four happy days bring in another moon-but O, methinks how slow this old moon wanes!

HIPPOLYTA. Four days will quickly steep themselves in night, four nights will dream away the time. And then the moon, shall behold the night.

THESEUS. Hippolyta, I wooed thee with my sword, and won thy love doing injuries. But I will wed thee in another key-With pomp, with triumph, and with reveling.

Enter Egeus, Hermia, Lysander, and Demetrius

EGEUS. Happy be Theseus, our renowned Duke!

THESEUS. Thanks, good Egeus. What's the news with thee?

EGEUS. Full of vexation come I, with the complaint against my daughter, Hermia. Stand forth Demetrius. This hath my consent to marry her. Stand forth Lysander. And, this man hath bewitched my child into loving him. I beg the ancient privilege of Athens. As she is mine, to dispose of her to this gentleman, (Pointing to Demetrius.) or to her death, according to our law.

THESEUS. What say you Hermia? Demetrius is a worthy gentleman.

HERMIA. So is Lysander!

THESEUS. In himself he is. But in your father's voice, the other must be held the worthier.

HERMIA. I would my father looked but with my eyes.

THESEUS. Rather your eyes must with his judgement look.

HERMIA. I do entreat your grace to pardon me. I know not by what power I am made bold. But I beseech your grace that I may know. The worst that may befall me in this case. If I refuse to wed Demetrius.

THESEUS. Either to die the death or marry who I say. For ever the society of men. Whether, if you yield not to your father's choice, you can endure the life of a nun.

HERMIA. So will I grow, so live, so die, my lord. (Kneel at his feet.)

THESEUS. (Take her hand to stand up.) Take time to pause, and by the next new moon- the sealing day, decide. For disobedience to thy father's will, upon that day prepare to die. Or else to wed Demetrius.

DEMETRIUS. Relent, sweet Hermia, and Lysander yield.

LYSANDER. You have your father's love, Demetrius. Let me have Hermia's.

EGEUS. Scornful Lysander! True, ha hath my love. And what is mine I do estate unto Demetrius.

LYSANDER. I am my lord, as well derived as he. My love is more than his. I am beloved of beauteous Hermia. Why should not I then prosecute my right?

THESEUS. I must confess that I have heard so much. And with Demetrius thought to have spoke thereof. But Demetrius come, and, come Egeus. You shall go with me, I have some private schooling for you both. Come Hippolyta, go along, go along, I must employ you in some business.

EGEUS. With duty and desire we follow you.

Exit all except Lysander and Hermia

LYSANDER. How now, my love? Why is your cheek so pale? How chance the roses there do fade so fast?

HERMIA. O spite! Too old to be engaged so young.

LYSANDER. Ay me, for aught that I could ever read the course of true love never did run smooth.

HERMIA. Oh cross! To choose by another's eyes! If then true love have never been crossed. But, it is customary cross, to teach patience.

LYSANDER. Therefore hear me Hermia. I have a widow aunt, a dowager of great revenue, and she hath no child, and she respects me as her only son. From Athens is her house, remote. There, gentle Hermia may I marry thee, and to that place Athenian law cannot pursue us. Steal forth thy father's house tomorrow night, and in the wood, there I will stay for thee.

HERMIA. My good Lysander, I swear to thee by Cupid's strongest bow, in that same place thou hast appointed me tomorrow truly will I meet with thee.

LYSANDER. Keep promise, Love. Look, here comes Helena.

Enter Helena

HERMIA. God speed, fair Helena. Wither away?

HELENA. Call you me fair? That 'fair' again unsay. Demetrius loves your fair- O happy fair!! O, teach me how you look, and with what art you sway the motion of Demetrius' heart.

HERMIA. I frown upon him, yet he loves me still.

HELENA. O that your frowns would teach my smiles such skill!

HERMIA. I give him curses, yet he gives me love.

HELENA. O that my prayers could such affection move!

HERMIA. The more I hate, the more he follows me.

HELENA. The more I love, the more he hateth me.

HERMIA. His folly, Helen, is no fault of mine.

HELENA. None but your beauty; would that fault were mine!

HERMIA. Take comfort. He no more shall see my face. Lysander and myself will fly this place.

LYSANDER. Helen, to you our minds we will unfold. Tomorrow night, when Phoebe doth behold, a time that lover's sleights doth still conceal- Through Athens gates have we devised to steal.

HERMIA. And in the wood where often you and I lie. There my Lysander and myself shall meet. And thence from Athens turn away our eyes. Farewell, sweet playfellow. Pray thou for us, and good luck thee thy Demetrius. Keep word, Lysander. From lovers food till morrow deep midnight.

LYSANDER. I will, my Hermia. Helena adieu.

Exit Hermia and Lysander

HELENA. (Alone.) How happy some o'er other some can be! Through Athens I am thought as fair as she. But what of that? Demetrius thinks not so. Love can transpose to form and dignity. Love looks not with the eyes, but with the mind, and therefore is winged cupid painted blind.

Act One
Scene Two
Fairy Forest, night

Enter Robin and Fairy

ROBIN. How now, spirit, whither wander you?

FAIRY. Over hill, over dale. Thorough bush, thorough brier, over park, over pale, thorough fire. I do wander everywhere. I serve the Fairy Queen. I must seek some dewdrops here, and hang a pearl in every cowslips ear. Farewell, thou lob of spirits. I'll be gone our Queen and all her elves come here anon.

ROBIN. The king doth keep his revels here tonight. Take heed the Queen come not within his sight. For Oberon is passing fell and wroth. Because that she, as her attendant, hath a lovely boy stol'n from an Indian king. She never had so sweet a changeling: And jealous Oberon would have the child. But she perforce withholds the loved boy, Crown him with flowers, and makes him all her joy.

FAIRY. Either I mistake your shape, or else you are that shrewd and knavish sprite called Robin Goodfellow. Are not you he? That frights the maidens of the villag'ry. Mislead night wanderers, laughing at their harm? Those that hobgoblin call you, and sweet puck, you do their work, and shall have good luck. Are not you he?

ROBIN. Thou speak'st aright. I am that merry wanderer of the night A merry hour was never wasted. But make room, fairy. Here comes Oberon.

Enter Oberon and Titiana (With fairies.)

FAIRY. And here my mistress. Would that he were gone.

OBERON. I'll met by moonlight, proud Titiana.

TITIANA. What, jealous Oberon? Fairies skip hence. (Fairies skip.)

OBERON. Tarry, rash wanton. Am I not thy Lord?

TITIANA. Then I must be thy Lady. But I know when thou hast stol'n away from fairyland. Why art thou here?

OBERON. Why indeed? Do you amend it then? It lies in you. Why should Titiana cross Oberon. I do but beg a little changeling boy to be my henchman.

TITIANA. Set your heart at rest. The fairyland buys not the child of me. His mother was a vot'ress of my order. But she, being mortal, of that boy did die. And for her sake do I rear up the boy. And for her sake I will not part with him.

OBERON. How long within this wood intend you stay?

TITIANA. Perchance till after Theseus' wedding day. If not, shun me, and I will spare your haunts.

OBERON. Give me that boy and I will go with thee.

TITIANA. Not for thy kingdom. Fairies away. (Fairies flutter away.) We shall chide downright if I longer stay.

Exit Titiana

OBERON. Well go thy way. Thou shalt not from this grove. My gentle Puck, come hither. Thou rememb'rest once I sat upon a dolphins back? And certain stars madly from their spears to hear the sea-maids music?

ROBIN. (Puck.) Yes my Lord.

OBERON. That very time I saw, but thou couldst not see young cupid's fiery shaft. Yet marked I where the bolt of Cupid fell. It fell upon a little western flower. Before, milk-white; now, purple with love's wound. And maidens call it love-in-idleness. Fetch me that flower. The herb I showed thee once. The juice of it on sleeping eyelids laid. Will make man or woman madly dote upon the next living creature that it sees. Fetch me this herb, and be thou here again.

ROBIN. I'll put a rope round the earth in forty.

Exit Robin, alone

OBERON. (Alone.) Having once this I'll Titiana when she is asleep, and drop this liquid in her eyes. The next thing she looks upon, be it lion, bear, wolf, or bull, she shall fall madly in love there with. And ere I take this charm from off her sight, I'll make her render up her page to me. But who comes here? I am invisible. And I will overhear this conference.

Enter Demetrius and Helena
Oberon overhears conversation.

DEMETRIUS. I love thee not, therefore pursue me not. Where is Lysander, and fair Hermia? The one I'll slay, the other slayeth me. Thou told'st me they were stol'n unto this wood. Because I cannot meet Hermia hence, get thee gone, and follow me no more.

HELENA. You draw me, you hard-hearted adamant. But yet you draw not iron: for my heart is true steel. Leave you your power to draw, and I shall have no power to follow.

DEMETRIUS. Do I entice you? Do I speak you fair? Or rather do I not in plainest truth tell you I do not nor I cannot love you?

HELENA. And even for that do I love you more. I am your spaniel, and Demetrius the more you beat me I will fawn on you.

DEMETRIUS. Tempt not too much the hatred of my spirit. For I am sick when I do look on thee.

HELENA. And I am sick when I look not on you.

DEMETRIUS. You do impeach your modesty too much.

HELENA. Your virtue is my privilege. Therefore I think I am not in the night. For you in my respect are all the world. Then how can it be said I am alone, when all the world is here to look on me.

DEMETRIUS. I will not stay thy questions. Let me go. Or if thou follow me, do not believe but I shall do thee mischief in the wood.

HELENA. We cannot fight for love as men may do; we should be wooed, and were not made to woo. I'll follow thee, and make a heaven of it. To die upon the hand I love so well.

Exit both

Act Two
Scene One
Fairy Forest, day

Enter Oberon, Robin

OBERON. Hast thou the flower? Welcome wanderer.

ROBIN. Ay, there it is.

OBERON. I pray thee give it me. I know a bank where there sleeps Titiana sometime of the night, lulled in these flowers with dance and delight. And with the juice of this I'll streak her eyes, and make her full of hateful fantasies. Then take thou some of it, and seek through this grove a disdainful youth. Anoint his eyes; but do it when the next thing he espies may be the lady! Thou shalt know the man by the Athenian garments he has on. More fond on her than she upon her love; and thou meet me ere the first cock crow.

ROBIN. Fear not, my lord, your servant shall do so.

Exit both

Act Two
Scene Two
Fairy Forest, night

Enter Titiana, Queen of Fairies and her train of fairies

TITIANA. Come, now a roundel and a fairy song. Sing me now asleep. Then to your offices, and let me rest. (She lies down.)

Fairies sing.

CHORUS. Lulla, lulla, lullaby. Lulla, lulla, lullaby. Never harm, nor spell nor charm. Come our lovely lady nigh. So good night, with lullaby.

Titiana sleeps, fairies sleep as well.

Enter Oberon
He drops the juice on Titiana's eyelids.

OBERON. What thou sees when thou dost wake. Do it for thy true love take. In thy eye that shall appear. When thou wak'st, it is thy dear. Wake when some vile thing is near.

Curtain closes.

Act Three
Scene One
Fairy Forest, day

Enter Lysander and Hermia

LYSANDER. Faie love, you faint with wand'ring in the wood. I have forgot our way. We'll rest us, Hermia, if you think it good. And tarry for the comfort of the day.

HERMIA. Be it so, Lysander. Find you out a bed. For I upon this bank will rest my head. (She lies down.)

LYSANDER. Amen, amen, to that fair prayer say I. Here is my bed, sleep give thee all his rest. (He lies down, they fall asleep.)

HERMIA. With half that wish the wisher's eyes be pressed.

Enter Robin

ROBIN. Through the forest have I gone, but Athenian found I none. Night and silence. Who is here? Weeds of Athens he doth wear. This is he my master said. Churl, upon thy eyes I throw. All the power this charm doth owe.
(He drops the juice on Lysander's eyelids.) When thou wak'st, let love forbid. Sleep his seat on thy lid. So, awake when I am gone. For I must now to Oberon.

Enter Demetrius and Helena running

HELENA. Stay, though thou kill me sweet Demetrius.

DEMETRIUS. I charge thee hence, and do not haunt me thus.

HELENA. O, wilt thou darkling leave me? Do not so.

DEMETRIUS. Stay, on thy peril. I alone will go.

HELENA. O, I am out of breath in this fond chase. Happy is Hermia, wheresoe'er she lies. For she hath blessed and attractive eyes. No, no; I am ugly as a bear. For beasts that meet me run away for fear. But who is here? Lysander, on the ground? Dead, or asleep? I see no blood. No wound. Lysander, if you live, good sir, awake.

LYSANDER. (Awaking.) Where is Demetrius? O, how fit a word. Is that vile name to perish on my sword?

HELENA. Do not say so, Lysander; say not so. What thou he love your Hermia? Lord, what thou? Yet Hermia still loves you; then be content.

LYSANDER. Content with Hermia? No, I do repent. The tedious minutes I have spent! Not Hermia but Helena I love. And reason says you are the worthier maid. And leads me to your eyes, where I o'erlook. Love's stories written in love's richest book.

HELENA. Wherefore was I to this keen mockery born? When at your hands did I deserve this scorn? Is't not enough, is't not enough, young man. That I did never-no nor ever can. Deserve a sweet look from Demetrius' eye. But fare you well. Perforce I must confess I thought you lord of more true gentleness.

LYSANDER. She sees Hermia. Hermia, sleep thou there. And never mayst thou come Lysander near. Of all be hated, but most of me. And all my powers, address your love and might to honour Helen, and to be her knight.

HERMIA. (Awaking.) Help me, Lysander, help me! Do thy best to pluck this crawling serpent from me. Ay me, for pity. What a dream was here? Lysander, look how I do quake with fear, Lysander what removed? Lysander, lord- What, out of hearing gone? No sound, no word? Alack, where are you ? Speak if you hear. Speak, of all loves. I swoon almost with fear. No? Then I will think you are not nigh. Either death or you I'll find immediately.

Act Three
Scene Two
Fairy Forest, day

TITIANA. (Awaking.) What angel wakes me from my flow'ry bed?

BOTTOM. The finch, the sparrow and the lark. Whose note full many a man doth mark. And dares not answer nay? (Singing.) I am on my way to a masked ball. Lalalalala (He has a donkey's head mask on.)

You must convey somehow that he is going to a masquerade ball.

TITIANA. I pray thee, gentle mortal, sing again. On the first view to say, to swear, I love thee.

BOTTOM. Methinks, mistress, you should have little reason for that. And yet, to say the truth, reason and love keep little company together nowadays.

TITIANA. Thou art as wise as thou art beautiful.

BOTTOM. Not so, neither; but if I had wit enough to get out of this wood, I have enough to serve mine own turn.

TITIANA. Out of this wood do not desire to go. Thou shalt remain here, whether thou wilt or no. And I do love thee. Therefore go with me. I'll give thee fairies to attend on thee, and they shall fetch thee jewels from the deep, and sing while thou on pressed flowers dost sleep.

Enter four fairies: Peaseblossom, Cob Webb, Mote, and Mustardseed

PEASEBLOSSOM. Ready.

COB WEBB. And I.

MOTE. And I.

MUSTARDSEED. And I.

ALL FOUR FAIRIES. Where shall we go?

TITIANA. Be kind and courteous to this gentleman. Feed him with apricots and dewberries.

MUSTARDSEED. And pluck the wings from painted butterflies to fan moonbeams from his sleeping eyes.

PEASEBLOSSOM. Hail mortal. (To Bottom.)

COB WEBB. Hail.

MOTE. Hail.

MUSTARDSEED. Hail.

BOTTOM. I cry your worship's mercy, heartily - I beseech your worship's name.

COBWEBB. Cobwebb.

TITIANA. (To fairies.) Come, wait upon him, lead him to my bower. Tie up my love's tongue: bring him silently. (Fetch him food, feed him, wait on him.)

Exit all

Act Three
Scene Three
Fairy Forest, day

Enter Oberon, King of the fairies

OBERON. I wonder if Titiana be awaked, then what it was that next came in her eye, which she must dote on in extremity.

Enter Robin Goodfellow

OBERON. Here comes my messenger. How now mad spirit?

ROBIN. My mistress with a monster is in love. While she was in her dull and sleeping hour, why she spied and walked straightway in love with a …. Donkey!

OBERON. This falls out better than I could devise; but hast thou yet latched the Athenian's eyes with the love juice? As I did bid thee do?

ROBIN. I took him sleeping; that is finished too, and the Athenian woman by his side, that when he waked of force she must be eyed.

Enter Demetrius and Hermia

OBERON. Stand close. This is the same Athenian.

ROBIN. This is the woman, but not this the man!

DEMETRIUS. O, why rebuke you him that loves you so? Lay breath so bitter on your bitter foe.

HERMIA. What's this to my Lysander? Where is he? Ah, good Demetrius, wilt thou give him to me?

DEMETRIUS. I had rather give his carcass to my hounds.

HERMIA. Out, dog; out, cur. Thou driv'st past the bounds of maiden's patience. Hast thou slain him then? O, once tell true; tell true, even for my sake. And hast thou killed him sleeping?

DEMETRIUS. You spend your passion on a misprised mood. I am not guilty of Lysander's blood. Nor is he dead, for aught that I can tell.

HERMIA. I pray thee, tell me then that he is well.

DEMETRIUS. And if I could, what should I get therefore?

HERMIA. A privilege never to see me more. And from thy hated presence part I so. See me no more, whether he be dead or no.

DEMETRIUS. There is no following her in this fierce vein. For debt that bankrupt sleep doth sorrow owe. Which now in some slight measure it will pay, if for his tender here I make some stay. (He lies down to sleep.)

OBERON. (To Robin.) What hast thou done? Thou hast mistaken quite. And laid the love juice on some true love's sight. Some true love turned, and not a false turned true? About the wood go swifter than the wind. And Helena of Athens look thou find. By some illusion see thou bring her here I'll charm his eyes against she do appear.

ROBIN. I go, I go-look how I go, swifter than arrow from the Tarter's bow. (He runs off.)

OBERON. (Casting a spell over Demetrius.) Flower of this purple dye, hit Cupid's archery, sink in apple of his eye. (He drops the juice on Demetrius' eyelids.) When his love he doth espy, let her shine as gloriously as Venus of the sky. When thou wak'st, if she be by, beg of her for remedy.

Act Four
Scene One
Fairy Forest, night

ROBIN. Captain of our fairy band, Helena is here at hand, (Pointing off stage.) And the youth mistook by me, pleading for a lover's fee. Lord, what fools theses mortals be.

OBERON. Stand aside. The noise they make, will cause Demetrius to awake.

ROBIN. Then will two at once woo one. That must needs sport, and those things do best please me that befall. (They stand apart.)

Enter Helena, Lysander following her

LYSANDER. Why should you think that I should woo in scorn? How can these things in me seem to scorn you, Bearing the badge of faith to prove them true.

HELENA. You do advance your cunning more and more. When truth kills truth- O devilish holy fray! These vows are Hermia's. Will you give her o'er?

LYSANDER. I had no judgement when to her I swore. Demetrius loves her, and he loves you not.

DEMETRIUS. (Awaking.) O Helen, goddess, perfect, divine! O, let me kiss thy hand! The princess of pure white.

HELENA. O spite! I see you are all bent to set against me for your merriment!

LYSANDER. You are unkind, Demetrius. Be not so. For you love Hermia; this you know. And here with all good will, with all my heart, In Hermia's love I yield you up my part.

HELENA. Never did mockers waste more idle breath.

DEMETRIUS. Lysander, keep thy Hermia. I will none. If e'er I loved her, all that love is gone. My heart to her but as guestwise sojourned and now to Helen is it returned, there to remain.

LYSANDER. Helen, it is not so.

DEMETRIUS. Look where thy love comes; yonder is thy dear.

HERMIA. Thou art not by mine eye, Lysander found, but why unkindly didst thou leave me so?

LYSANDER. Why should he stay whom love doth press to go? The hate I bare thee made me leave so?

HERMIA. You speak not as you think. It can not be!

HELENA. (Whisper to the side, to audience.) Now I perceive they have conjoined all three? To fashion this false sport in spite of me.

HERMIA. I am amazed at your passionate words. I scorn you not. It seems you scorn me.

HELENA. Have you not set Lysander, as in scorn to follow me? And made your other love Demetrius spurn me with his foot?

HERMIA. I understand not what you mean by this?

HELENA. Ay do! Make mouths upon me when I turn my back. Death or absence soon shall remedy.

LYSANDER. Stay gentle Helena, hear my excuse. My love, my life, my soul, fair Helena!

HELENA. O excellent!

LYSANDER. Helen, I love thee; by my life I do.

DEMETRIUS. (To Helena.) I say I love thee more than he can do.

Hermia cries and paces.

LYSANDER. Prove it! (To Demetrius.)

DEMETRIUS. Quick come!

HERMIA. Lysander where to tends all this? (She takes him by the arm.)

LYSANDER. Away you!

DEMETRIUS. No, no sir yield. You are tame man, go!

LYSANDER. (To Hermia.) Hang off. Let loose. Or I will shake thee from me like a serpent.

HERMIA. Why have you grown so rude? What change is this sweet love?

LYSANDER. Thy love? Out! O hated potion, hence. (He realizes a spell was cast on him.)

Curtain

Act Four
Scene Two
Forest

Enter Oberon and Robin, attendants

OBERON. This is thy negligence. (To Robin.)

ROBIN. Believe me king of shadows, I mistook. Did you not tell me I should know the man by his Athenian garments? (Points to Lysander.)

OBERON. Thou seest these lovers seek a place to fight. We must right this wrong upon these men. Crush this herb into Lysander's eyes to take all error away. When they next wake shall seem a dream to them. Back to Athens shall the lovers hence. And while in this do thee employ I'll go to my queen and beg back the Indian boy. And then I will her charmed eye release from the monsters view and all shall be in peace.

ROBIN. My fairy lord, this must be done with haste. (He starts the spell.) Up and down, up and down. I will lead them up and down. Here comes one now.

ATTENDANT. Goblin, lead them up and down.

ATTENDANT. Here comes one.

Enter Lysander

LYSANDER. Where art thou Demetrius? Speak thee now!

ROBIN. (Pretending to be Demetrius, hiding.) Here, villain, drawn and ready. Where art thou?

LYSANDER. (Looking confused.) I will be with thee straight. (Drawing his sword.)

ROBIN. (Hiding.) Follow me then.

Lysander follows voice.

DEMETRIUS. Lysander speak again. Thou run away. Thy coward. Speak. In some bush?

ROBIN. (Hiding, shifting position.) Thou coward, telling the bushes that thou lookst' for wars? Draw a sword on thee.

DEMETRIUS. Yea, art thou there?

ROBIN. Follow my voice. And wilt not come.

LYSANDER. What is thou there? When I come where he calls, then he is gone. The villain is much lighter heeled than I. I followed fast but did he fly. Here will rest me. (He lies down.)

DEMETRIUS. Where art thou now? Thou runnest before me, shifting every place. Faintness overpower me. (He lies down.)

Enter Helena

HELENA. Oh weary night. So that I may back to Athens by daylight. (She yawns and lies down.)

ROBIN. (Coming out of the forest.) Yet but three? Come one more. Two of both kinds makes up four.

Enter Hermia

ROBIN. Here she comes curst and sad. Cupid is a knavish lad.

HERMIA. Never so weary, never so in, Woe! I can no further crawl, no further go. (She lies down.)

ROBIN. On the ground sleep sound. I'll apply to your eye, gentle lover remedy. (He drops juice on Lysander's eyelids.) When thou wak'st thou tak'st true delight in the sight of thy former lady's eye. Jack shall Jill, naught shall go ill.

Act Four
Scene Three
Fairy Forest, day

Enter Titiana, Bottom, (With a donkey's head on.) fairies

TITIANA. (To Bottom.) Come, sit thee down upon thy flow'ry bed. And kiss thy large ears. (Kisses his ears.) Wilt thou hear some music my sweet love?

BOTTOM. I have a good ear in music. Let's have some.

Music plays, and fairies dance and sing.

TITIANA. Or sweet love desir'st to eat? Some peanuts per chance?

BOTTOM. Methinks I would rather a handful of two dried peas.

TITIANA. Sleep thou now, fairies be gone. (She waves her hand.) They fall asleep.

Enter Robin and Oberon (Meeting.)

OBERON. Welcome. Good Robin. See'st thou sweet sight? I do begin to pity. I will undo this hateful vex of her eyes. (He drops the juice in her eyelids.) Be as thou wast won't to be. See as thou wast won't to see. Now wake my Titiana, wake you, my sweet queen.

TITIANA. (Yawns.) My Oberon, what visions have I seen. Methinks I was in love with a fool!

OBERON. There lies your love.

TITIANA. How came these things to pass? O, how mine eyes do hate this donkey now.

OBERON. Silence awhile. Robin do take off his head.

Robin takes donkey head off Bottom.

OBERON. Sound music. (Music plays.) Come my queen, take hands with me. (Oberon and Titiana dance.)

ROBIN. Hark fairy king, I do hear the morning lark sing.

TITIANA. Come, my lord and in our flight tell me how it came this night to find these mortals sleeping on the ground. (Pointing to mortals.)

Enter Theseus, Egeus, Hippolyta and train (Horns sound.)

THESEUS. Go, go one of you, go find them!

EGEUS. My lord, methinks this is my daughter here asleep. And this is Lysander, this Demetrius, and this Helena.

THESEUS. No doubt they rose up early. But speak Egeus, is this not the day that Hermia should give answer of her choice?

EGEUS. It is, my lord.

THESEUS. Go with the huntsman wake them with their horns. (Horns blow.)

The lovers all stand up.

THESEUS. Good morrow friends. Saint Valentine is past.

LYSANDER. Pardon my lord. (They all kneel.)

THESEUS. I pray you all stand up. (Lovers stand.) (To Demetrius and Lysander.) I know you two are rival enemies. To sleep by hate and fear no pain?

LYSANDER. My lord, I shall reply amazedly. I cannot truly say how I came here. I came with Hermia hither, to be gone from Athens where we might marry.

EGEUS. (To Theseus.) Enough, my lord.

DEMETRIUS. (To Theseus.) My lord, fair Helen told me of their travel. I, in fury followed them. Fair Helena in fancy followed me, but my lord, my love is to Hermia. To her, my lord I will for evermore be true.

THESEUS. Fair lovers, you are fortunately met, for in temple by and by with us these couples shall eternally be knit. Away with us to Athens. Three and three, We'll hold a feast in great happiness, come Hippolyta. (All leave.)

Music plays.

Curtain closes and opens to all three couples getting married.

THESEUS. Here come the lovers full of joy and mirth. Joy gentle friends. Accompany your hearts. Come now, what dances shall we have. (He dances with his wife.)
All three couples dance. Wedding celebration.

The End

Macbeth

Cast of Characters

First Witch

Second Witch

Third Witch

Duncan (Ghost of Duncan.)*

Malcolm

Sergeant

Lennox

Ross

Macbeth

Banquo

Lady Macbeth

Messenger (s)

Fleance

Macduff

Servant (s)

Donalbain

Angus

Attendant (s)

Doctor

Townspeople

Musicians

Guests

Server (s)

Stage Manager

Stage hands

Narrator

Curtains

Porter (s)

* you can have two separate people for this character

Macbeth

Enter Narrator

NARRATOR. Macbeth is a man overcome by his ambition, so he commits murder even though he can foresee the tragic consequences of his own actions. At first when he thinks about killing Duncan and overthrowing his kingdom for the crown, he thinks he can murder him without any personal consequences. He would like to see the deed, murder, vanish from time itself. He imagines he can do this. But his reason tells him, he is causing his own destruction.

(Beginning of play.)

Act One
Scene One

Scotland England
A desert place
Thunder and lightning

Enter three witches

FIRST WITCH. When shall we three meet again? In thunder, lightning, or in rain?

SECOND WITCH. When the hurlyburly's done, when the battle's won.

THIRD WITCH. That will be ere the set of sun.

FIRST WITCH. Where the place?

SECOND WITCH. Upon the heath.

THIRD WITCH. There to met with Macbeth.

FIRST WITCH. I come, graymalkin!

SECOND WITCH. Paddock calls.

THIRD WITCH. Anon!

ALL WITCHES. Fair is foul, and foul is fair, hover through the fog and filthy air. (I had them dance and skip around the cauldron.)

Exit all

Act One
Scene Two
A camp near Forres

Enter Duncan, Malcolm, Lennox, meeting a bleeding sergeant

DUNCAN. What bloody man is that?

MALCOLM. This sergeant. Who like a good and hardy solider fought 'gainst my captivity? Hail brave friend!

SERGEANT. Worthy to be a rebel. But all's too weak. For brave Macbeth-well deserves that name.

DUNCAN. O valiant cousin! Worthy gentleman!

SERGEANT. Discomfort swells. Mark, king of Scotland, Mark, began a fresh assault.

DUNCAN. Dismay'd not this our captains, Macbeth and Banquo?

SERGEANT. Yes. I cannot tell- But I am faint; my gashes cry for help.

DUNCAN. So well thy words become thee as thy wounds; they smack of honour both. Go get him surgeons.

Exit sergeant

Enter Ross

MALCOLM. Who comes here? The worthy thane of Ross.

LENNOX. What a haste looks through his eyes! So should he look that seems to speak things strange.

DUNCAN. Whence camest thou worthy thane?

ROSS. From Fife, great king; where the Norweyan banners flout the sky. And fan our people cold. The thane of Cawdor, began a dismal conflict. Point against point, arm against arm. The victory fell on us.

DUNCAN. Great happiness!

ROSS. That now, ten thousand dollars to our general use. (Shows pouch full of money.)

DUNCAN. No more that thane of Cawdor shall deceive. Go pronounce his present death, and his former title greet Macbeth.

ROSS. I'll see it done.

DUNCAN. What hath he lost, noble Macbeth hath won.

Exit all

Act One
Scene Three
A heath
Thunder and lightning

Enter the three witches

FIRST WITCH. Where hast thou been, sister?

SECOND WITCH. Killing swine.

THIRD WITCH. Sister, where thou?

FIRST WITCH. A sailor's wife had chestnuts in her lap, and munched, and munched, and munched! Give me, quoth: and, like a rat without a tail, I'll do, I'll do, and I'll do. (Motions as if to steal away something.)

SECOND WITCH. I'll give thee a wind.

FIRST WITCH. Thou'rt kind.

THIRD WITCH. And I another.

FIRST WITCH. I myself have all the other; I' the shipman's card. I will drain him dry as hay; sleep shall neither night nor day. Hang upon his penthouse lid; he shall live a man forbid. Look what I have.

SECOND WITCH. Show me, show me. (Drums heard off in the distance.)

FIRST WITCH. Have I a pilot's thumb. Wreck'd as homeward he did come. (Drums.)

THIRD WITCH. A drum, a drum. Macbeth doth come.

Dancing in a circle around the cauldron.

ALL WITCHES. The weird sisters, hand in hand, posters of the sea and land. Thus do go about, about. Thrice to thine, and thrice to mine. And thrice again, to make up mine. Peace! The charm's wound up.

Enter Macbeth and Banquo

MACBETH. So foul and a fair day I have not seen.

BANQUO. How far is't call'd to Forres? What are these, so wither'd and so wild in their attire. Upon her skinny lips: you should be women, and yet your breath forbid me to interpret that you are so.

BANQUO. Speak, if you can: what are you?

FIRST WITCH. All hail Macbeth! Hail to thee, thane of Glamis!

SECOND WITCH. All hail , Macbeth! Hail to thee, thane of Cawdor!

THIRD WITCH. All hail, Macbeth, that shall be king hereafter!

BANQUO. Good sir why do you start, and seem to fear, things that do sound so fair? My noble partner you greet with present grace and great prediction. Speak then to me, who neither beg nor fear your favors nor your hate.

Witches throw glitter.

FIRST WITCH. Hail!

SECOND WITCH. Hail!

THIRD WITCH: Lesser than Macbeth, and greater.

SECOND WITCH. Not so happy, yet much happier.

THIRD WITCH. Thou shalt get kings, though be none. So all hail, Macbeth and Banquo!

FIRST WITCH. Banquo and Macbeth, all hail!

MACBETH. Stay, you imperfect speakers, tell me more. By Sinel's death I know I am thane of Glamis; but how of Cawdor? The thane of Cawdor lives. Say from whence you owe this strange intelligence? Speak, I charge you?

Witches Vanish. (Fog machine, I ran the fog machine every time they were on stage.)

BANQUO. The earth hath bubbles as the water has, and these are of them. Whither are they vanished?

MACBETH. Into the air, and what seemed like bodies melted as breath into the wind. Would they had stayed.

BANQUO. Were such things here as we do speak about? Or have we eaten on the insane root.

MACBETH. Your children shall be kings.

BANQUO. You shall be king.

MACBETH. And thane of Cawdor too: went it not so?

BANQUO. To the self same tune and words. Who's here?

Enter Ross

ROSS. The king hath happily received, Macbeth, he has heard the news of thy success. He bade me, from him, call thee thane of Cawdor, for it is thine.

BANQUO. What, can the devil speak true?

MACBETH. The thane of Cawdor lives: why do you dress me, in borrow'd robes?

ROSS. He bears that life which he deserves to lose. He labor'd in his country's wreck, I know not; but treasons capital, confess'd and proved, have overthrown him.

MACBETH. Thanks for your pains. The greatest is behind. (To Banquo.) Do not hope your children shall be kings, when those that gave the thane of Cawdor to me promised no less to them?

BANQUO. (To Macbeth.) That, trusted home, might enkindle you unto the crown, besides the thane of Cawdor. But 'tis strange. Cousin, a word, I pray you.

MACBETH. Two truths are told, I thank you gentlemen. This supernatural soliciting cannot be ill; cannot be good. Commencing is a truth? I am thane of Cawdor. My thought is smothered in surmise, and nothing is but what is not. If chance will have me king, why, chance may crown me. Without my stir.

BANQUO. New honors come upon him.

MACBETH. Come what may. Time and the hour runs through the roughest day.

BANQUO. Worthy Macbeth, we stay upon your leisure.

MACBETH. Give me your favor; my dull brain was wrought with things forgotten. Let us toward the king. Let us speak our free hearts each to other.

BANQUO. Very gladly.

MACBETH. Till then, enough, come friends.

Exit

Act One
Scene Four

Trumpets sound
Forres the palace

Enter King Duncan, Malcolm, Donalbain, Lennox and attendants

DUNCAN. Is execution done on Cawdor? Are not those in commission yet return'd?

MALCOLM. My liege, they are not yet come back. But I have spoke with one that saw him die; he died as 'twere a careless trifle. (Hand out as if to push away.)

DUNCAN. There's no art to find the mind's construction in the face; he was a gentleman on whom I built an absolute trust. (Enter Macbeth, Banquo, and Ross.) O worthiest cousin! The sin of my in gratitude was heavy on me. More is thy due than more all can pay.

MACBETH. The service and the loyalty I owe, in doing it, pays itself.

DUNCAN. (To Banquo.) Welcome hither; I have begun to plant thee, and will labour to make thee full of growing.

BANQUO. There if I grow, the harvest is your own.

DUNCAN. Our eldest, Malcolm, whom we name hereafter the Prince of Cumberland.

MACBETH. The rest is labour, which is not used for you. The hearing of my wife with your approach, so humbly take my leave.

DUNCAN. My worthy Cawdor!

MACBETH. The Prince of Cumberland! That is a step on which I must fall down, or else o'erleap.

DUNCAN. True, worthy Banquo; he is so full of valiant. It is a banquet to me. Let's after him.

Trumpets.
Exit All

Act One
Scene Five
Macbeth's castle-Inverness

Enter Lady Macbeth

LADY MACBETH. (Reading a letter.) I have met three witches. They have more in them than mortal knowledge. I tried to ask them more, but they vanished. They all hailed me, "Thane of Cawdor," by which title these weird sisters saluted me. Hail, king that shalt be! This I have to deliver to thee, my dearest partner. Lay it to thy heart and farewell.

Enter a messenger

LADY MACBETH. What is your tidings?

MESSENGER. The king comes here to-night.

LADY MACBETH. Thou'rt mad to say it. Is not thy master with him? Who have inform'ed you for preparation?

MESSENGER. So please you, it is true; our thane is coming. One of my fellows had the speed with him.

LADY MACBETH. (Pacing.) Give him tending. He brings great news. (Messenger exits.) Come, you spirits make thick my blood. Come thick night. Nor heaven to peep through the blanket of the dark. Hold, hold!

Enter Macbeth

LADY MACBETH. Great Glamis! Worthy Cawdor! Greater than both all hail hereafter! Your letter has transported me beyond the ignorant past. I feel now the future in instant.

MACBETH. My dearest love, Duncan comes here to-night.

LADY MACBETH. And when goes hence?

MACBETH. To-morrow, as he purposes.

LADY MACBETH. O, never shall sun that morrow see! Your face, my thane, is as a book where men may read strange matters. He that is coming be the serpent. He must be provided for. I shall dispatch tonight's business.

MACBETH. We shall speak further.

LADY MACBETH. Only look up clear. To alter favor ever is to fear. Leave all the rest to me.

Exit

Act One
Scene Six
In front of Macbeth's castle
Woodwind instruments sound

Enter Duncan with, Malcolm, Donalbain, Banquo, Lennox, Macduff, Ross, Angus, and attendants

DUNCAN. This castle hath a pleasant seat, the air sweetly smells.

BANQUO. This guest summer. I have observed the air is delicate.

Enter Lady Macbeth

DUNCAN. See, see, our honour'ed hostess! The love that follows us sometime is our trouble.

LADY MACBETH. All our service in every point twice done, and then done double. Your majesty loads our house. Come rest your feet.

DUNCAN. Where's the thane of Cawdor? He rides well. He hath arrives home before us. Fair and noble hostess, we are your guests to-night.

LADY MACBETH. Have theirs, themselves, and what is theirs, inside.

DUNCAN. Give me your hand. Take me to mine host. We love him highly. By your leave, hostess.

Exit

Act One
Scene Seven
Macbeth's castle
Torches lit

Enter servants with dishes of food and service and pass over stage
Enter Macbeth

MACBETH. (Alone on stage.) If it were done when 'tis done, then 'twere well it were done quickly. If th' assassination Could trammel up the consequence and catch. But in these cases this even-handed justice commends the ingredients of our poison'd chalice to our own lips. Who should against his murderer shut the door. Not bear the knife myself. Duncan hath been so meek. His tears shall drown the wind and fall on others. Might be the be-all and the end-all.

Enter Lady Macbeth

LADY MACBETH. How now! What news! He has almost supp'd. Why have you left the chamber?

MACBETH. Hath he ask'd for me?

LADY MACBETH. Know you not he has?

MACBETH. We will proceed no further in this business. He hath honour'd me of late; and I have bought golden opinions from all sorts of people.

LADY MACBETH. Art thou afeared to be the same in thine own act and valour. As thou art in desire? Wouldst thou live a coward in thine own esteem? Letting 'I dare not,' wait upon 'I would,' like a poor cat I' the cage?

MACBETH. Prithee peace! I dare do all that may become a man. Who dares do more is none.

LADY MACBETH. What beast was it then that made you break this enterprise to me? Be so much more the man?

MACBETH. If we should fall?

LADY MACBETH. We fail! And we'll not fail. When Duncan is asleep- What cannot you and I perform upon the unguarded Duncan? His spongy officers, shall bear the guilt of our great quell.

MACBETH. Bring forth men, nothing but males. When we have marked with blood those sleepy two, men of his own chamber, and use their daggers, that they have not done it?

LADY MACBETH. Who dares receive it other, as we shall make our grief's and clamour roar upon his death.

MACBETH. I am settled to this terrible feat. Away, and mock the time with fairest show. False face must hide what the false heart doth know.

Act Two
Scene One
Court of Macbeth's castle-Inverness

Enter Banquo, and Fleance, he is bearing a torch before him

BANQUO. How goes the night boy?

FLEANCE. The moon is down; I have not heard the clock.

BANQUO. And she goes down at twelve.

FLEANCE. I take tis later, sir.

BANQUO. Hold, take my sword. The candles are all out. A heavy summons lies like lead upon me. And yet I would sleep.

Enter Macbeth, and a servant holding a torch

BANQUO. Give me my sword. Who's there?

MACBETH. A friend

SERVANT. All's well.

BANQUO. What sir, not yet at rest? The king's a bed. He hath been in unusual pleasure and sent forth some riches to you. This diamond he greets your wife with. All's well. I dreamt last night of the three weird sisters: To you they have show'd some truth.

MACBETH. I think not of them, we would spend it in some words upon that business if you would grant the time.

BANQUO. At your kind'st leisure.

MACBETH. If you shall be counsell'd.

MACBETH. Good repose the while!

BANQUO. Thanks, sir: the like to you!

Exit Banquo and Fleance

MACBETH. (To the servant.) Go bid thy mistress, when my drink is ready. She strike upon the bell. Get thee to bed. (Exit servant.) Is this a dagger which I see before me? (He sees a dagger.) The handle toward my hand? Come, let me clutch thee. I have thee not, and yet I see thee still. Art thou not, fatal vision, sensible. A dagger of the mind a false creation? I see thee still. And on thy blade gouts of blood. Which was not so before. There's no such thing. Is it the bloody business which informs me thus to mine eyes. (A bell rings.) I go, and it is done: The bell invites me. Hear it not Duncan, for it is a bell. That summons thee to death.

Act Two
Scene Two
Court of Macbeth's castle

Enter Lady Macbeth

LADY MACBETH. What hath quench'd them hath given me fire. Duncan must be done now! Macbeth must go and kill him now! The doors to his chambers are open. I have drugged the servants that watch the king, one cannot tell whether they are alive or dead! Hark! Peace!

MACBETH. (Inside castle.) Who's there? What Ho?

LADY MACBETH. Alack, I am afraid they have awaked. And 'tis not done; the attempt and not the deed confounds us. Hark! I laid their daggers ready; he could not miss'em. He had not resembled my father as he slept, I hadn't done it.

Enter Macbeth, carrying bloody daggers, obviously upset

LADY MACBETH. My husband.

MACBETH. I have done the deed. Did thou not hear a noise?

LADY MACBETH. I heard the owl scream and the crickets cry: did not you speak?

MACBETH. When?

LADY MACBETH. Now.

MACBETH. As I descended?

LADY MACBETH. Ay.

MACBETH. Hark! Who lies in the second chamber?

LADY MACBETH. Donalbain.

MACBETH. (Looking at his hands.) This is a sorry sight.

LADY MACBETH. A foolish thought, to say a sorry sight.

MACBETH. There's one did laugh in his sleep, and one cried, Murder!

LADY MACBETH. These deeds must not be thought after these ways; so it will make us mad.

MACBETH. Me thought I heard a voice cry 'sleep no more.' I Macbeth shall sleep no more.

LADY MACBETH. Who was it that thus cried? Go get some water and wash this filthy witness from your hand. Why did you bring these daggers from the place? They must lie there; go carry them, and smear the sleepy groomsmen with blood.

MACBETH. I'll go no more. I am afraid to think what I have done. Look on it again, I dare not.

LADY MACBETH. Give me the daggers! The sleeping and the dead are but pictures.

Exit Lady Macbeth, knocking is heard

MACBETH. Whence is that knocking?

Enter Lady Macbeth

LADY MACBETH. My hands are of your color, but I shame to wear a heart so white. (Knocking within.) I hear a knocking. (Knocking is heard.) Hark! I hear more knocking.

MACBETH. To know my deed, twere best not know myself. (Knocking within.) Wake Duncan with my knocking! If only I could!

Act Two
Scene Three
Macbeth's castle

Knocking within.

Enter a porter

PORTER. Here's a knocking indeed! (Knocking within.) Knock! Knock! Who's there? Is it the devil? O come in. (Knocking within.) Knock! Knock! Knock! Who's there? Never at quiet! What are you? (Knocking within.) Anon! Anon! I pray you, remember the porter. (Opens the gate.)

Enter Lennox and Macduff

MACDUFF. Is thy master stirring? (Enter Macbeth.) Our knocking has awaked him, here he comes.

LENNOX. Good morrow, noble sir.

MACBETH. Is the king stirring, worthy thane?

LENNOX. Not yet.

MACDUFF. He did command me to call on him. I have almost let an hour slip by.

MACBETH. I'll bring you to him.

MACDUFF. I know this is a joyful trouble to you. But yet 'tis one.

MACBETH. This is the door.

MACDUFF. I'll make so bold a call.

Exit Macduff

LENNOX. Goes the king hence today?

MACBETH. He does. He did appoint so.

LENNOX. The night has been unruly. We heard strange screams of death. Some say the earth was feverous and did shake.

MACBETH. 'Twas a rough night.

LENNOX. I'm too young to remember anything like that.

Enter Macduff, running, upset

MACDUFF. O horror, horror, horror! Tongue nor heart can explain!

MACBETH AND LENNOX. What's the matter?

MACDUFF. Confusion now hath made his masterpiece. A murder hath broke out!

MACBETH. What is't you say? The life of whom?

LENNOX. Mean you his majesty?

MACDUFF. Approach his chamber, and destroy your sight. Do not bid me speak. See, and then speak yourselves. (Exit Macbeth and Lennox.) Awake! Awake! Ring the alarm bell. Murder and treason! Malcolm awake and look upon death itself! Up, up, and see! Malcolm! Banquo! Ring the bell!

Enter Lady Macbeth
Bell rings.

LADY MACBETH. What's the business? That such a hideous trumpet calls us? Speak, speak!

MACDUFF. O' gentle lady! 'Tis not for you to hear what I can speak. The news in a woman's ear, would murder as it fell.

Enter Banquo

MACDUFF. O Banquo, Banquo, our royal master's murdered!

LADY MACBETH. Woe, alas! What, in our house?

BANQUO. Too cruel anywhere. Macduff, I pray thee contradict thyself, and say it is not so.

Enter Macbeth, Lennox, and Ross

MACBETH. Had I but died an hour before this chance. I had lived a blessed time.

Enter Malcolm and Donalbain

DONALBAIN. What is amiss?

MACBETH. You are, and do not know it. The spring of your royal blood is stopped.

MACDUFF. Your royal father's been murdered.

MALCOLM. Oh, by whom?

LENNOX. Those of his chamber, as it seems, had done it. Their hands and faces were all badged with blood. So were their daggers, which unwiped we found under their pillows. They stared, and we were distracted No man's life was to be trusted with them.

MACBETH. Oh, yet I am sorry of my fury. That I did kill them.

MACDUFF. Wherefore did you so?

MACBETH. Who can be wise and furious in a moment? No man. Here lay Duncan. Steeped in their daggers. Who could refrain?

LADY MACBETH. Help me hence ho!

Act Three
Scene One

Servers carrying food on stage.
Musicians playing.
Guests arriving.

Enter Banquo

BANQUO. Thou has it now, king, Cawdor, Glamis. As the weird women promised. May they not be my oracles as well.

MACBETH. (Pointing to Banquo.) Here's our chief guest. Tonight we hold a solemn supper.

BANQUO. Let your highness command upon me, to which my duties.

MACBETH. Ride you this afternoon?

BANQUO. Ay, my good Lord.

MACBETH. Fail not our feast.

BANQUO. My Lord, I will not.

Exit Banquo

Act Three
Scene Two
Party

MACBETH. Sweet remembrance! Now, good digestion wait on appetite, and health to all!

LENNOX. Health to all! May it please your highness. (Drinks toast.)

Enter Ghost of Duncan, only Macbeth sees him

MACBETH. Here had we now all the nobility of Scotland gathered.

ROSS. His absence sir, Duncan, lays blame upon his promise. Please your majesty, sit.

MACBETH. The tables full. (He sees the ghost in the chair.)

LENNOX. Here is a place reserved, sir.

MACBETH. Where?

LENNOX. Here my good lord. What is it that moves your highness? (He points to an empty chair, but the ghost is in it.)

MACBETH. Which of you has done this?

LORDS. What my good lord?

MACBETH. (To ghost of Duncan.) Thou canst not say I did it. Never shake thy gory head at me.

ROSS. Gentleman, rise. His highness is not well. (They all think Macbeth is crazy.)

LADY MACBETH. Sit, worthy friends. My lord is often thus and has been since his youth. Pray you, keep seat. The fit is momentary, he will be well again. You shall offend him and extend his passion. (Aside to Macbeth.) Are you a man?

MACBETH. Ay, and a bold one that dare look on that which might appall the devil.

LADY MACBETH. O proper stuff! Shame itself! Why do you make such faces? When all is done, you'll see your looking upon an empty stool.

MACBETH. Please, see there! Behold! Look! Lo! How say you? Why, what care I? If thou canst' nod. Speak too.

Exit ghost

MACBETH. If I stand here, I saw him.

LADY MACBETH. Fie, for shame!

MACBETH. Ay, murder hath been performed too terrible for the ear. But now he rises again. And he pushes me from my stool. This is more strange than such a murder is.

LADY MACBETH. My worthy lord, your noble friends do lack you.

MACBETH. I do forget. I have a strange infirmity, which is nothing to those that know me. Come, love and health to all. Then I shall sit down. Give me some drink. Fill full.

LORDS. Our duties and the pledge.

They all drink.

MACBETH. (Seeing the ghost once again.) What man dare, I dare. Approach me. Take a shape, or be alive again. (Staring at the ghost, which is nothing, but an empty chair to all.) Hence, horrible shadow! Unreal mockery, hence!

Exit ghost

LADY MACBETH. You have displaced the mirth, broke the good meeting, made us all in disorder.

MACBETH. Can such things be? Overcome us like a summer cloud? You make me strange.

ROSS. What sights my lord?

LENNOX. Good night, and better health attend his majesty!

LADY MACBETH. A kind good night to all1

Exit all, except Lady Macbeth and Macbeth

MACBETH. It will have blood they say. Blood will have blood. Stones have been known to move.

LADY MACBETH. You lack the season of all natures, sleep.

MACBETH. Come we'll sleep. We are yet but young in deed.

Act Four
Scene One

A cavern, in the middle a boiling cauldron, thunder.

Three witches enter, dance around cauldron.

FIRST WITCH. Thrice the tawny cat mewed.

SECOND WITCH. Thrice, and once the hedgehog whined.

THIRD WITCH. My spirit friend cries, ‘tis time, ‘tis time.

FIRST WITCH. Round about the cauldron dancing, in the poisoned entrails throw. Toad, that under cold stone days and night has thirty-one. (Throws a toad into the cauldron.)

ALL WITCHES. Double, double toil and trouble, fire burn, and cauldron bubble.

SECOND WITCH. Fillet of a fenny snake, (Holds up a snake.) in the cauldron boil and bake. Eye of newt and toe of frog, wool of bat and tongue of dog. Adder’s fork and blind-worm’s sting, lizard’s leg and owlet’s wing, for a charm of powerful trouble, like a fiery-broth boil and bubble. (Throws snake in cauldron.)

ALL WITCHES. Double, double toil and trouble, fire burn and cauldron bubble.

Enter Macbeth

MACBETH. How now, you secret, black, and midnight hags? What is it you do?

ALL WITCHES. A deed without a name.

MACBETH. I conjure you by that which you profess. But answer me. Even till destruction sicken, answer me to what I ask.

FIRST WITCH. Speak.

SECOND WITCH. Demand.

THIRD WITCH. We'll answer.

FIRST WITCH. Say, if th' hadst rather hear it from our mouths.

MACBETH. Call 'em. Let me see 'em.

FIRST WITCH. Pour in sow's blood that hath eaten grease.

ALL WITCHES. Come, high or low; thyself and office show.

Enter ghost of Duncan, thunder

MACBETH. Tell me, thou unknown power-

FIRST WITCH. He knows thy thought. Hear his speech but say thou naught.

GHOST OF DUNCAN. Macbeth! Macbeth! Macbeth! Beware Macduff he sides with the crowd of your murdered king. Dismiss me! Enough!

MACBETH. Then live, Macduff. What need I fear of him? He is not a worthy opponent.

ALL WITCHES. Seek to know more?

MACBETH. I am satisfied.

Music.
The Witches dance and then vanish. (Fog.)

MACBETH. Where are they? Gone? Come in, without there.

Enter Lennox

LENNOX. What's your grace's will?

MACBETH. Saw you the weird sister's?

LENNOX. No, my lord.

MACBETH. Came they not you?

LENNOX. No, indeed, my lord.

MACBETH. I did hear the galloping of horses. Who was't that came by?

LENNOX. 'Tis two or three, my lord, that bring you word Macduff is fled to England.

MACBETH. Fled to England?

LENNOX. Ay, my good lord.

MACBETH. The castle of Macduff I will surprise. This deed I'll do before this purpose cool. But no more visions. Where are these gentleman? Come, bring me where they are.

Exit

Act Five
Scene One
Doctor in room in castle

Enter Lady Macbeth and servant, with a taper

DOCTOR. How came she by that light. What is it she does now? Look how she rubs her hands.

LADY MACBETH. Yet here's a spot.

DOCTOR. Hark she speaks. I will set down what comes from her, to satisfy my remembrance the more strongly.

LADY MACBETH. Out darn spot! Out, I say! One- two- why then tis time to do it. This is murky. Fie, my lord! What need we fear who knows it, when none can call power to accompany it? Yet who would have thought the old man to have had so much blood in him?

DOCTOR. Do you mark that?

SERVANT. She has spoke what she should not, I am sure of that. Heaven knows what she has known.

LADY MACBETH. Here's the smell of blood still. All the perfumes of Arabia will not sweeten this little hand. Oh, oh, oh! (Upset.)

DOCTOR. What a sigh is there! The heart is sorely charged.

LADY MACBETH. Wash your hands, put on your nightgown, look not so pale! I tell you yet again, Duncan's buried. He cannot come out one's grave.

DOCTOR. Even so?

LADY MACBETH. To bed, to bed! Ther's knocking at the gate. Come, come, come, come, give me your hand! What's done cannot be undone. To bed, to bed, to bed!

Exit Lady Macbeth

DOCTOR. Will she go now to bed?

SERVANT. Directly.

DOCTOR. Whiles I see lives, do better upon them Unnatural deeds do breed unnatural troubles. Infected minds to their deaf pillows. God, forgive us all! Look, after her. I think but dare not speak.

SERVANT. Good night, good night dear doctor.

Exit both

Act Five
Scene Two
Castle

MACBETH. The way to dusty death. Out, out brief candle. Life's a walking shadow, a poor player, signifying nothing.

Enter a messenger.

MESSENGER. Gracious my lord, I should report that which I say I saw, But know not how to do't.

MACBETH. Well, say sir.

MESSENGER. As I did stand my watch upon the hill, I thought the wood began to move.

MACBETH. Liar!

MESSENGER. I saw a moving grove!!!

MACBETH. If thou speak'st false, upon the next tree shall thou hang alive. Come! Ring the alarm bell. Fear not!

Exit

Men come bells ringing.
Macbeth is tied to a tree, have these players stay on stage so they can carry him off later.

MACBETH. They have tied me to a stake. I cannot fly. Am I to fear, or none.

MACDUFF. Tyrant show your face! If someone other than me kills you, the ghost of Duncan wll haunt me still.

MACBETH. Why should I play the Roman fool and die. On mine own sword? Whiles I see lives, do better upon them.

MACDUFF. Turn, round, turn!

MACBETH. Of all the men else I have avoided thee. But get thee back. My soul is too much charged with blood of thine already.

MACDUFF. I have no words. My voice is in my sword. Thou bloody villain.

They fight.

MACDUFF. Yield thee, coward. And live to be the show and gaze at thee all the time.

MACBETH. I will not yield. Yet I will try the last. Before my body I throw my warlike shield. Lay on, Macduff, and be him that first cries, Hold enough!

Macbeth is slain.
Carried off stage by players that tied him to the tree.

Enter Malcolm, Lennox, Donalbain, Ross, with drums

MALCOLM. Then he is dead?

MACDUFF. Ay, and brought off the field. Your cause of sorrow must not be measured by his worth, for then it hath no end.

LENNOX. He's worth more sorrow, and that I'll spend for him.

MACDUFF. Hail, king! For so thou art! The time is free. Hail, King of Scotland!

MALCOLM. We shall not spend a large expense of time before we reckon with your several loved ones and make us even with you. That fled snares of watchful tyranny, producing forth cruel ministers. So, thanks to all at once and to each one, whom we invite to see us crowned at Scone. Hail King of Scotland!

ALL. Hail King of Scotland!

THE END

Made in the USA
Lexington, KY
26 June 2013